Reviving Rural News helps readers see the value and role of community and rural news, and helps the people running those newsrooms see the dire need for thoughtful experimentation, which, by the way, works. This book shows that we – readers, communities, and journalists – all have a stake in the survival of local news and a role to play in that transformation.

– **Kristen Hare,** *Poynter*

Local news is one of the most valuable forms of journalism, yet it is ironically also the least economically secure. Drawing on a rich data set, *Reviving Rural News* offers a sharply written explanation of why this problem persists, and, more importantly, puts forward a compelling argument for how to solve it. The result is an invaluable contribution to both journalism studies and practice that not only provides a novel solution to one of journalism's most distressing problems, but also a template for how journalists and journalism scholars can – and should – work together.

– **Jake Nelson,** *University of Utah*

Reviving Rural News

Based on extensive research into weekly rural publishers and rural readers, *Reviving Rural News* demonstrates that a new financial approach to community journalism is urgently needed and viable.

This book provides historical context for the state of local news, examines the influence of journalistic identity and boundaries that have prevented change, and offers practical guidance on how to adapt the financial strategies of weekly newspapers to the habits of modern readers. Findings are grounded in robust data collection, including surveys, focus groups, and a year-long oral history study of a small weekly newspaper group in the United States. A new model known as Press Club is presented as a template via which memberships, events, and newsletters can better engage community journalism with its audiences and create a more sustainable path for the future.

Reviving Rural News will be of interest to advanced students and researchers of local, community, and rural journalism as well as practitioners looking to bring about real-world change in journalism organizations.

Teri Finneman is an associate professor of journalism at the University of Kansas, USA. She is a journalism historian who also studies local news. She coedited *Social Justice, Activism and Diversity in U.S. Media History*. She is the founder of the Journalism History podcast.

Nick Mathews is an assistant professor at the School of Journalism, University of Missouri, USA. He studies local and rural news and information ecosystems. He often seeks to represent the audience, translating their lived experiences for news organizations to help those news organization's stability and viability in their communities.

Patrick Ferrucci is an associate professor and chair of the Department of Journalism at the University of Colorado, USA. His research is in media sociology and primarily concerns itself with how shifting notions of "organization" in journalism lead to influence on journalism practice. He is the author of *Making Nonprofit News: Market Models, Influence and Journalism Practice*, and coeditor of *The Institutions Changing Journalism: Barbarians Inside the Gates*.

Disruptions: Studies in Digital Journalism

Series editor: Bob Franklin

Disruptions refers to the radical changes provoked by the affordances of digital technologies that occur at a pace and on a scale that disrupts settled understandings and traditional ways of creating value, interacting and communicating both socially and professionally. The consequences for digital journalism involve far reaching changes to business models, professional practices, roles, ethics, products and even challenges to the accepted definitions and understandings of journalism. For Digital Journalism Studies, the field of academic inquiry which explores and examines digital journalism, disruption results in paradigmatic and tectonic shifts in scholarly concerns. It prompts reconsideration of research methods, theoretical analyses and responses (oppositional and consensual) to such changes, which have been described as being akin to 'a moment of mind-blowing uncertainty'.

Routledge's book series, *Disruptions: Studies in Digital Journalism*, seeks to capture, examine and analyse these moments of exciting and explosive professional and scholarly innovation which characterize developments in the day-to-day practice of journalism in an age of digital media, and which are articulated in the newly emerging academic discipline of Digital Journalism Studies.

The Disputed Freedoms of a Disrupted Press
Ivor Shapiro

Reviving Rural News
Transforming the Business Model of Community Journalism in the US and Beyond
Teri Finneman, Nick Mathews and Patrick Ferrucci

For more information about this series, please visit: www.routledge.com/Disruptions/book-series/DISRUPTDIGJOUR

Reviving Rural News

Transforming the Business Model of Community Journalism in the US and Beyond

Teri Finneman, Nick Mathews, and Patrick Ferrucci

LONDON AND NEW YORK

First published 2024
by Routledge
4 Park Square, Milton Park, Abingdon, Oxon OX14 4RN

and by Routledge
605 Third Avenue, New York, NY 10158

Routledge is an imprint of the Taylor & Francis Group, an informa business

British Library Cataloguing-in-Publication Data
A catalogue record for this book is available from the British Library

Library of Congress Cataloging-in-Publication Data
Names: Finneman, Teri Ann, author. | Mathews, Nick, author. | Ferrucci, Patrick, author.
Title: Reviving rural news : transforming the business model of community journalism in the US and beyond / Teri Finneman, Nick Mathews and Patrick Ferrucci.
Description: London ; New York : Routledge, 2024. | Series: Disruptions: studies in digital journalism | Includes bibliographical references and index.
Identifiers: LCCN 2023052393 (print) | LCCN 2023052394 (ebook) | ISBN 9781032539768 (hardback) | ISBN 9781032539775 (paperback) | ISBN 9781003414582 (ebook)
Subjects: LCSH: Rural journalism--United States--History. | Journalism, Regional--Economic aspects--United States. | Journalism--Economic aspects--United States. | Newspaper publishing--United States. | American newspapers--History.
Classification: LCC PN4888.C7 F56 2024 (print) | LCC PN4888.C7 (ebook) | DDC 071/.3--dc23/eng/202311
LC record available at https://lccn.loc.gov/2023052393
LC ebook record available at https://lccn.loc.gov/2023052394

ISBN: 978-1-032-53976-8 (hbk)
ISBN: 978-1-032-53977-5 (pbk)
ISBN: 978-1-003-41458-2 (ebk)

DOI: 10.4324/9781003414582

Typeset in Times New Roman
by KnowledgeWorks Global Ltd.

Contents

Acknowledgments

The authors thank the William Allen White School of Journalism and Mass Communications, the Southern Newspaper Publishers Association Foundation, the Kansas Press Association, the South Dakota Newspaper Association, the North Dakota Newspaper Association, and the Nebraska Press Association for their funding and support throughout this project. We also thank Joey and Lindsey Young and their team for opening up their newsrooms and agreeing to be part of this experiment.

1 Introduction

Rural Journalism in Crisis

Patrick Ferrucci and Teri Finneman

What needs to be done to save local news?

This question assumed an urgent importance during the COVID-19 pandemic amidst an already growing news desert crisis. Despite the fact that many weekly newspapers turned into 24-7 operations to serve public demand during the global health crisis, newsrooms still faced the threat of closure prompted by financial freefall (Finneman and Thomas, 2021; Hare, 2021). The advertising-centric business model that had been crumbling for over two decades collapsed at a time when news was needed most, with more than 100 U.S. newsrooms closing (Hare, 2021). The strain on journalists was evident in a series of oral histories conducted in 2020 with 28 publishers, editors, and reporters at weekly and regional newspapers in the middle of the United States (Finneman, Mari, and Hare, 2021). Throughout the 700 pages of transcripts capturing their stories, newsroom leaders were worried about losing their family legacy newspapers, experiencing stress under the burden of editorial and business upheaval, and scrambling to bring in new revenue sources.

A particularly noteworthy interview was with Joey Young, owner of Kansas Publishing Ventures based in Newton, Kansas. At the time, he was a 35-year-old owner of five publications with about 30 employees in south central Kansas. In March 2020, his information technology staff had to reinforce the company's website due to a tremendous spike in reader traffic seeking pandemic news. Yet Young found himself constantly stressed about money. Young, who is known for speaking directly, admitted the pandemic's toll on his news business increased his gray hair and the amount he was drinking. "Early on in the pandemic, like, I spent a lot of nights physically not sleeping," he said.

> It's made it hard to sleep sometimes 'cause you don't know what tomorrow brings and you've worked really hard, and you've sacrificed a lot, and you've put all of your personal finances into a company, and you were doing really well before the pandemic and now you just don't know what tomorrow is.
>
> (Finneman, 2021)

DOI: 10.4324/9781003414582-1

The oral histories articulating the experiences of Young and others in the project, along with additional reports of the financial distress industrywide, made one thing abundantly clear: Academia had failed the journalism industry. Standing by as mere passive recorders and commentators of the industry's collapse over the last two decades had done little, if anything, to reverse the decline of newspapers. Even after the Great Recession in the United States between 2008 and 2010, no significant progress was made to alter the newspaper industry's business model that had long been faltering due in part to revenue declines perpetuated by the internet and social media. No urgent action occurred despite the fact that newspaper revenues fell by 23% between 2007 and 2009 and despite a warning that 25% of all newsroom jobs that existed in 2001 would disappear by the end of 2009 (State of the News Media, 2009). Beyond the periodic and completely unrealistic calls for public funding of news, academic work did little to help the situation. With the pandemic serving as yet another critical incident decimating the industry in 2020, one thing became clear: A serious academic-industry intervention was needed to help local news.

Although the majority of journalism in the United States is produced by community newspapers, weeklies are frequently overlooked in broader discussions of journalism that is focused more on the major metro dailies and chain ownership. The views of people in "flyover country" in the Midwest have long been ignored or glossed over by national media and political culture due in part to the more intensive work involved in undertaking rural outreach and a dismissal of the importance of rural opinions. *Reviving Rural News* specifically aims to share the voices of and create solutions for communities with fewer than 10,000 people. These rural populations tend to have no one but their weekly newspaper to provide them with local information, thereby increasing the urgency of stabilizing the financial future of community journalism.

The goal of this book is to provide a new business model template for community newspapers. Over the course of 18 months, three universities partnered with four newspaper associations to generate data to inform a revenue theory. Young's flagship newspaper, *Harvey County Now*, would ultimately pilot the experiment between June 2022 and June 2023 (Figure 1.1). In addition to maintaining its current revenue model, *Harvey County Now* adopted membership, e-newsletter, and event strategies with the hope these would bolster its bottom line. These changes impacted the entire staff – co-owners Joey and Lindsey Young, editor Adam Strunk, ad director Bruce Behymer, and a few reporters (Figure 1.2). Over the course of the first year, the new model called Press Club shifted as real-world realities intermingled with academic theory. Early results indicate short-term successes in financing journalism with $10,000 in initial profit, as well as long-term successes in building stronger connections with their community. Just as important, the experiment resulted in a noticeable psychological shift among the journalism staff themselves as their initial hesitation about change grew increasingly into confidence throughout the course of their oral histories captured over 14 months.

Figure 1.1 Lindsey Young and Bruce Behymer work from the *Harvey County Now* office in downtown Newton, Kansas, in June 2023. The staff agreed to take part in a one-year business model experiment for weekly newspapers. Courtesy of Teri Finneman.

Figure 1.2 Adam Strunk (front) and Joey Young get some work done before attending the June 2023 Press Club event. This book explores the staff's creation of Press Club as a strategy for increasing revenue and community relationships at rural newspapers. Courtesy of Teri Finneman.

Before providing an explanation of how this Press Club business model formed and outlining detailed guidance for implementation, it is important to examine the context that led to the present conditions. Journalism history has played a role in cementing the industry's current status, as has rigid adherence to journalistic identity and boundaries, declining rural populations, and technological barriers. Furthermore, the problem of declining local news and news deserts goes beyond the United States, creating a global demand for solutions.

The History of How We Got Here

A full accounting of the history of journalism's business model would fill a book in itself, particularly if international models are also examined. Therefore, this is not intended as a comprehensive analysis but prefers to offer a lay version of developments to help understand why the industry operates like it does today.

The business model used by the U.S. newspaper industry has roots that first sprouted in 1833. To provide context, Andrew Jackson was president and Samuel Morse was working on the telegraph. Before the 1833 penny press revolution, U.S. newspapers in the 1700s and early 1800s were expensive at 6 cents. Initially focused on international and business news, newspapers evolved into partisan operations backed by political parties (Shaw and Slater, 1985). The partisan press catered to wealthy white male readers who could vote and were, consequently, too costly and unappealing for a broader audience (Daly, 2012). A 23-year-old set out to change that. Benjamin Day launched the first successful penny newspaper, the *New York Sun*, in the United States in 1833 about two decades after the same experiment in England (Sloan, 2011). Rejecting the jurisdiction of political parties, the penny press era emphasized cheap news for a mass audience that was free of partisan control. Perhaps best recognized for their ties to newsboys selling papers on the streets, these penny papers served those "who had never before considered a daily newspaper important to their well-being" (Tucher, 1994, p. 16). In addition to "the appealing price of the *Sun* [that] put it in the reach of all classes of readers," the newspaper's focus on human interest, crime, and local news set it apart and made it a circulation leader (Sloan, 2011, p. 127). Technological advances in printing capability, the railroad, and the telegraph further eased the distribution of news in the first half of the 1800s (Daly, 2012).

The news industry began to see that the new model of mass circulation and advertising "meant political independence and editorial individualism" (Bird, 2003, p. 58). Famed *New-York Tribune* publisher Horace Greeley, a penny press pioneer himself, latched onto political independence as a transformative moment for press freedom, thereby connecting the business model with the First Amendment (Stewart, 2012). The concept of the penny press took time to expand outside New York City, however. Bird (2003) notes it took another

30 years to be adopted in Virginia, while Kaplan (1995) writes the *Detroit Evening News* introduced a 2-cent paper in 1873 that innovated the 5-cent market there at the time. Even though newspapers moved at different speeds of transformation, the period from the early 1830s to the 1860s in general was a time when the news industry was willing to innovate "in news collection, in business practices, and in content" (Huntzicker, 1999, p. 164). James Gordon Bennett of the *New York Herald* would lead the charge "that a newspaper editor ought to make a great deal of money" and "like all the penny editors, he was experimenting, finding his way, driven by a multitude of ideas" (Tucher, 1994, p. 20).

This new business model to serve the masses at an affordable price came with "considerable pressure," however, to maintain circulation sales (Daly, 2012, p. 59). It also enhanced the role of advertising. Although advertising in U.S. newspapers dates back to 1704 (Lee, 1937), the industry's reliance on this revenue steadily grew following the decline of the partisan press and its political funding. In 1847, about 11 million ads ran in a few thousand U.S. newspapers and generated about $1 million in revenue. By the end of the century, there were 350 million ads in 16,000 publications generating nearly $96 million (Dicken-Garcia, 1989; Presbry, 1929). By 1929, U.S. newspapers gleaned 74% of their revenue from advertising compared to 44% in 1879 (Lee, 1937).

The 1880s and 1890s – also referred to as the yellow journalism era – were another critical time in the shaping of the newspaper industry, due in large part to the influence of publishers Joseph Pulitzer and William Randolph Hearst. From the newsroom side, there was an increased emphasis on local news, particularly in relation to "sensation, crusade, expose, scandal, stunt, and sob story" (Daly, 2012, p. 126). Newspapers became increasingly visual with enhanced page design, illustrations, and photos as technology improved. Pulitzer's *New York World* thrived with community engagement strategies, such as encouraging readers to donate change to pay for a base for the Statue of Liberty and hosting a reader contest for how many days it would take Nellie Bly to go around the world (Daly, 2012). Industrialization and the rise of products influenced the launch of women's pages to attract women to the newspaper and the accompanying advertising (Voss, 2023). The influence of Pulitzer and Hearst can still be seen in the present even though the "detached, impartial, yet authoritative treatment of news" (Campbell, 2006, p. 6) modeled by competing publisher Adolph Ochs at the *New York Times* ultimately became the industry's norm.

While most think of the news side in relation to the yellow journalism era, the business strategies implemented during this time arguably had the bigger impact. Daly (2012) describes this as a time when newspapers "transition[ed] from a stand-alone shop to a giant industrial enterprise" (p. 120) as "mass production, mass marketing, and mass communication joined forces in a new dynamic" (p. 118). Pulitzer created a new standard of setting ad rates based on circulation and "ordered his staff to cooperate with advertisers in designing larger and more attractive ads" (p. 120). This was a key turning point for newspaper economics as the amount of space given to advertising soon equaled the amount given to news (Daly, 2012).

Signs of trouble for the business model – and the industry's failure to deal with change – began to emerge soon after World War II, however. As David Davies outlines in *The Postwar Decline of American Newspapers, 1945–1965*, issues for journalism began long before the internet was invented: "Buoyed by profits during most of the early postwar years, publishers failed to act when business and society pressures challenged newspapers to adapt" in the 1950s and 1960s (p. ix). These pressures included the rise of television as a competitor, circulation stagnation, rising costs to operate, increasing corporate ownership, and adherence to "objectivity" in a heightened political climate of McCarthyism and civil rights. Davies argues that the challenges in the postwar years "sent the daily newspaper industry on a decline that continues to this day." Newspapers were slow to adapt to technological improvements, such as moving from letterpress to offset printing despite the new innovation being a cheaper alternative (Davies, 2006). Metro dailies were not proactive in the face of competition for advertising and consumer attention from television and new suburban newspapers. Prices for newspapers rose from 3 cents to 5 cents as growth in chain ownership put more focus on profitability over the newsroom (Davies, 2006). Although statistics from the era illustrate strong profitability and circulation, Davies argues the numbers are deceptive. In reality, although daily newspaper circulation rose, it lagged behind population growth. Furthermore, consolidations and mergers killed dozens of newspapers each year, a fact masked by an increase in suburban dailies (Davies, 2006). As a whole, Davies concluded, "newspapers as a group were slow to respond to the problems facing journalism" (p. 129).

As the news industry neared the end of the 20th century, not much changed concerning the industry's preferred advertising-focused business model, but the ownership of many organizations changed (McManus, 1994). By the 1990s and into the early 2000s, the journalism ecosystem saw itself consumed by large chains and conglomerates, the kind of companies which expected the historical robust profit margins employed by newspapers to continue indefinitely (Cohen, 2015). However, as the 2000s began with the explosion of the internet, print advertising revenue began to rapidly dwindle – exacerbated further by the financial crisis of 2007 and 2008 – leaving even the most financially privileged news organizations with lessening profits. This led many conglomerates and chains to cut staff sizes across the country, beginning a rapid decline in the number of employed journalists in the United States.

While traditional print and broadcast newsrooms suffered through this decline, the beginning of the 21st century saw increased experimentation with business models, particularly in digitally native journalism. This included an influx of nonprofit journalism (Ferrucci, 2019; Konieczna, 2018), more organizations hosting events for profit (Larson, 2015), mergers with public news organizations (Belair-Gagnon, Nelson & Lewis, 2019), more membership models (Price, 2020), and foundation funding (Ferrucci & Nelson, 2019). While many of these revenue streams proved successful for a number of news organizations, pivoting to new revenue streams has been more difficult for rural journalism organizations.

The Norms of Journalism

In the early 1970s, management scholar Chris Argyris conducted an extended ethnographic investigation into the *New York Times*. Argyris' main goal "was to discover what must be done to create newspapers that are self-examining and self-regulating" (Argyris, 1974, p. ix). As a scholar of organizational change, Argyris wanted to understand through participant observation what processes needed altering and what norms should be shifted to create a better, more efficiently run business. What the scholar did not understand, and he implies this in the book's conclusion, is the many unseen but well-established normative professional practices that undergird the field of journalism, the very practices that an organization would more often than not fail to change. For example, Ryfe (2009) detailed the efforts of a new editor at a large metropolitan daily who, among other changes, attempted to end the beat system at the newspaper, the very normative practice that media sociologists such as Tuchman (1978) found to be absolutely essential to the practice of journalism. In Ryfe's study, the journalists revolted against these changes and, eventually, the editor was removed. Ryfe (2009) concluded the editor's reforms would fundamentally alter what it meant to be a journalist in the newsroom and that "professional identity is tightly bound to practice, reporters can quickly feel at sea when one of their key practices (like routine interactions with officials at public agencies) is disrupted" (p. 212). In effect, Argyris (1974) concluded something similar and contended that effective organizational change "requires continual self-examination and self-renewal … the communication media (and specifically journalism has) shown little interest in such activities" (p. x).

While there is broad consensus currently that professional identity in journalism is "seemingly shifting" (Ferrucci & Vos, 2017, p. 868), or liquid (Jaakkola et al. 2015), there is still little debate that said identity is defined, both inside and outside the field of journalism, through the normative processes that are intrinsically part of the practice (Singer, 2015; Vos & Ferrucci, 2018). These behaviors or actions or norms, such as objectivity, are so connected to the identity of journalists that making change is difficult. This simple fact can be extrapolated to any notion of changing the revenue model for journalism in the United States.

For example, for decades, scholars looked to public funding as a potential financial panacea for journalism, but also a normative imperative, separating what they view as a public service from the market. However, much research from both the academy and the industry shows that journalists themselves are against this, primarily because of the normative notion of journalism as the fourth estate, a watchdog that could not bark if funded by the other three estates (e.g., Kovach & Rosenstiel, 2021). In effect, any change to the revenue model of a journalistic organization would result in ripple effects (or perceived ripple effects) on practice, which could violate normative assumptions, which then would more than likely result in some kind of failure. This type of question needs to be explored within the context of geography and system. In the United States, because of journalism's historic ties to the market, public funding is often, as mentioned, shunned. But in other countries without this historical relationship, that is not the case. However, regardless of geography, the precarious funding of journalism is currently a global issue.

An International Problem

While the scope of this book concerns itself primarily with the United States and the results may not be generalizable in any context (although we believe they are), the problem of funding journalism is global. The financial precariousness of journalism is something affecting newsrooms regardless of geography or, even, market model. Advertising revenues for journalism are decreasing globally, resulting in potentially negative implications for democracy across the world (Picard, 2010).

We are living through a time when journalism struggles to disseminate the news while "established business models continue to be disrupted by digital transformation and a global pandemic has brought into sharp focus the need for trusted, local news that keeps citizens informed and holds local power to account" (Harte & Matthews, 2022, p. 2). Research illustrates that news deserts are increasing across the world, from numerous parts of Africa (Madrid-Morales, Rodríguez-Amat & Lindner, 2023), to areas around Scandinavia (Sjøvaag, 2022), to Brazil (da Silva & Pimenta, 2020), to Spain (Negreira-Rey, Vázquez-Herrero & López-García, 2023), and to Australia (Magasic & Hess, 2021).

The significant point here is that while this project is decidedly American, the goal of the experiment described within this book aims to help alleviate an overwhelmingly international problem. The hope is that what is learned from the research focused on the Press Club model developed here and examined in this book can be implemented and tested around the globe: That these insights – and the overall success found – can inspire similar work across geographic domains.

Project Overview

Understanding that rural publishers are risk averse, skeptical of advice outside of their peers, and operate in cultures different than those of metro newsrooms, the book relies heavily on input from rural publishers and rural readers. This book's findings are grounded in a robust data collection that includes three primary methodologies. First, we utilize two surveys, one of 106 rural news organization owners (a total of 176 papers) and the other of 414 rural residents across the central United States. These surveys examine how the two groups consider various funding models for journalism. Second, we organized four focus groups with nearly two dozen newsroom leaders. These discussions underscored the ramifications of digital disruption – including financial demands and growing audience demands for more frequent news updates (especially during the COVID-19 pandemic) – as well as news leaders' thoughts on how to better adjust to these new demands. Third, we employ a year-long oral history study of a small weekly newspaper group willing to share its success and failures in launching a new business model. This aspect of our research includes a series of interviews with the news organization's owners and employees. Oral history is critical for the ability to publicly discuss details of the research subjects involved and to publicly preserve all of the data as opposed to the more confidential restrictions associated with ethnography and semi-structured interviews. Journalists want to see real-world examples, not anonymous framing, and oral history provides an extra layer of transparency for future researchers.

Chapter 2 examines the uniqueness of rural news. Although the majority of journalism in the United States is produced by community newspapers, weeklies are frequently overlooked in broader discussions of journalism that are focused more on the major metro dailies as well as chain ownership. This chapter provides an overview of what is rural news? What makes weekly newspapers different from the rest of the journalism industry? What are their unique opportunities and challenges? The chapter also incorporates discussions of the theory of disruptive innovation, role identity, and organizational culture that help to explore and explain how rural newsrooms function.

Chapter 3 focuses on publishers and their views of the industry's business model and financial options. Before we began our organizational intervention, we conducted a survey of rural newspaper publishers in the central United States about potential revenue streams. We also conducted focus groups with newsroom leaders and explored the same economic issues. This chapter highlights the fears/concerns that newspaper publishers have that prevent them from changing their business model.

Chapter 4 offers insight from rural readers and what they are looking for in weekly newspapers. We discuss the results of our second survey of a representative sample of residents in the Central States area of the United States. This quantitative and qualitative data focused on how readers would financially support local news. This chapter makes a unique contribution in its efforts to directly hear from rural consumers of news.

Chapter 5 details the intervention we oversaw at our news organization participant and tells the evolving story through oral history interviews with its employees. We discuss how we decided on the business model changes, how the organization implemented them, and the opportunities and challenges that occurred during the yearlong experiment from June 2022 to June 2023. This chapter explores how the changes affected both the economic viability of the organization, but also the practices and, particularly, community engagement endeavors undertaken through the invention of Press Club. We sum up the added economic benefits of the intervention, but also the time commitment needed for implementation and continued execution.

Chapter 6 extends beyond our massive case study and begins exploring the ramifications of our intervention through both a practical journalism perspective and the lens of digital journalism studies. We outline and empathize with the difficulties brought by digital disruption, but also believe in a positive way forward. We outline our recommendations to the rural news organization ecosystem globally, but also offer a roadmap for the future theoretical study of rural news, particularly its intersection with economic forces affecting the field.

Ultimately, *Reviving Rural News* illustrates the disconnect between readers in the present day and rural publishers clinging to old-school approaches to journalism. Rigid defenses of journalistic boundaries – as well as journalistic identity that intertwine business and personal failure – present challenges for moving past a financial model that has dominated journalism for centuries. Yet *Reviving Rural News* also demonstrates how change is possible as we chronicle a newspaper group's transition to a new model known as Press Club. After decades of struggling to determine a new business model – and in some cases, barely managing to survive with the current one – the COVID-19 pandemic must serve as a historical turning point that newspapers can no longer delay adopting new financial strategies. Journalism organizations around the world must confront a new, more perilous financial foundation in the aftermath of continued digital disruptions in the past three decades. For smaller news organizations with limited staff and resources, this is an even larger challenge. This book brings together 18 months of extensive research with rural newspaper publishers and rural readers to examine a path forward for funding community journalism.

References

Argyris, C. (1974). *Behind the front page: Organizational self-renewal in metropolitan newspapers*. Jossey-Bass Incorporated Pub.

Belair-Gagnon, V., Nelson, J. L., & Lewis, S. C. (2019). Audience engagement, reciprocity, and the pursuit of community connectedness in public media journalism. *Journalism Practice, 13*(5), 558–575.

Bird, S. (2003). Heralding economic and political independence: Danville, Virginias newspaper editors adopt James Gordon Bennett's penny press model during the Civil War. *American Journalism, 20*(4), 55–82. https://doi.org/10.1080/08821127.2003.10677963

Campbell, W.J. (2006). *The year that defined American journalism: 1897 and the clash of paradigms*. Routledge.

Cohen, N. S. (2015). Entrepreneurial journalism and the precarious state of media work. *South Atlantic Quarterly, 114*(3), 513–533.

da Silva, C. E. L., & Pimenta, A. (2020). Historical and contemporary perspectives. In A. Gulyas & D. Baines (Eds.), *The Routledge companion to local media and journalism*. Routledge.

Daly, C. (2012). *Covering America: A narrative history of a nation's journalism*. University of Massachusetts Press.

Davies, D. (2006). *The postwar decline of American newspapers, 1945–1965*. Praeger.

Dicken-Garcia, H. (1989). *Journalistic standards in nineteenth century America*. University of Wisconsin Press.

Ferrucci, P. (2019). *Making nonprofit news: Market models, influence and journalistic practice*. Routledge.

Ferrucci, P., & Nelson, J. L. (2019). The new advertisers: How foundation funding impacts journalism. *Media and Communication, 7*(4), 45–55.

Ferrucci, P., & Vos, T. (2017). Who's in, who's out? Constructing the identity of digital journalists. *Digital Journalism, 5*(7), 868–883.

Finneman, T. (2021). For community newspapers in Kansas, merging saved money and benefited readers. *Poynter*. https://www.poynter.org/reporting-editing/2021/for-community-newspapers-in-kansas-merging-saved-money-and-benefited-readers/

Finneman, T., Mari, W., & Hare, K. (2021, March 2). The essential workers. *Poynter*. https://www.poynter.org/the-essential-workers/

Finneman, T., & Thomas, R. J. (2021). "You had to be reporting constantly": COVID-19's impact on U.S. weekly newspapers' journalistic routines. *Newspaper Research Journal, 42*(3), 330–345. https://doi.org/10.1177/07395329211030390

Hare K. (2021, November 30). More than 100 local newsrooms closed during the coronavirus pandemic. *Poynter*. https://www.poynter.org/locally/2020/the-coronavirus-has-closed-more-than-25-local-newsrooms-across-america-and-counting/

Harte, D., & Matthews, R. (2022). *Reappraising local and community news in the UK*. Routledge.

Huntzicker, W. (1999). *The popular press:1833–1865*. Greenwood Press.

Jaakkola, M., Hellman, H., Koljonen, K., & Väliverronen, J. (2015). Liquid modern journalism with a difference: The changing professional ethos of cultural journalism. *Journalism Practice, 9*(6), 811–828.

Kaplan, R. (1995). The economics of popular journalism in the gilded age. *Journalism History, 21*(2), 65–78. https://doi.org/10.1080/00947679.1995.12062411

Konieczna, M. (2018). *Journalism without profit: Making news when the market fails*. Oxford University Press.

Kovach, B., & Rosenstiel, T. (2021). *The elements of journalism: What newspeople should know and the public should expect* (revised and updated 4th edition). Crown.

Lee, A.M. (1937). *The daily newspaper in America*. The Macmillan Company.

Madrid-Morales, D., Rodríguez-Amat, J. R., & Lindner, P. (2023). A computational mapping of online news deserts on African news websites. *Media and Communication, 11*(3).

Magasic, M., & Hess, K. (2021). Mining a news desert: The impact of a local newspaper's closure on political participation and engagement in the rural Australian town of lightning ridge. *Australian Journalism Review, 43*(1), 99–114.

McManus, J. H. (1994). *Market-driven journalism: Let the citizen beware?* Sage Publications.

Negreira-Rey, M.-C., Vázquez-Herrero, J., & López-García, X. (2023). No people, no news: News deserts and areas at risk in Spain. *Media and Communication, 11*(3).

Pew Charitable Trusts. (2009). State of the news media. https://www.pewtrusts.org/en/research-and-analysis/reports/2009/03/16/the-state-of-the-news-media-2009

Picard, R. G. (2010). A business perspective on challenges facing journalism. In D. A. L. Levy & R. K. Nielsen (Eds.), *The changing business of journalism and its implications for democracy* (pp. 17–24). Reuters Institute for the Study of Journalism. https://reutersinstitute.politics.ox.ac.uk/sites/default/files/research/files/The%2520Changing%2520Business%2520of%2520Journalism%2520and%2520its%2520Implications%2520for%2520Democracy.pdf

Presbry, F. (1929). *History and development of advertising*. Doubleday.

Price, J. (2020). How to feed The Ferret: Understanding subscribers in the search for a sustainable model of investigative journalism. *Journalism, 21*(9), 1320–1337.

Ryfe, D. M. (2009). Broader and deeper: A study of newsroom culture in a time of change. *Journalism, 10*(2), 197–216.

Shaw, D., & Slater, J.W. (1985). In the eye of the beholder? Sensationalism in American press news, 1820–1860. *Journalism History, 12*(3–4), 86–91. https://doi.org/10.1080/00947679.1985.12066610

Singer, J. B. (2015). Out of bounds: Professional norms as boundary makers. In M. Carlson & S. C. Lewis (Eds.), *Boundaries of journalism: Professionalism, practices, and participation* (pp. 21–36). Routledge.

Sjøvaag, H. (2022). *The markets for news: Enduring structures in the age of business model disruptions*. Routledge.

Sloan, W. (2011). *The media in America* (8th ed.). Vision Press.

Stewart, D. (2012) Freedom's vanguard: Horace Greeley on threats to press freedom in the early years of the penny press. *American Journalism, 29*(1), 60–83. https://doi.org/10.1080/08821127.2012.10677814

Tucher, A. (1994). *Froth & scrum*. University of North Carolina Press.

Tuchman, G. (1978). *Making news: A study in the construction of reality*. Free Press.

Vos, T. P., & Ferrucci, P. (2018). Who am I? Perceptions of digital journalists' professional identity. In S. Eldridge II & B. Franklin (Eds.), *The Routledge handbook of developments in digital journalism studies* (pp. 40–52). Routledge.

Voss, K. (2023). *Vivian Castleberry: Challenging the traditions of women's roles, newspaper content, and community politics*. Lexington Books.

2 The Uniqueness of Rural News

Patrick Ferrucci

When academics or even major industry actors such as the Pew Foundation discuss "the news industry," they too often only refer to large newspapers or "the 'elite metro dailies' that are the most high-profile newspapers in their cities and states" (Reader, 2018, p. 32). However, when surveying the entire news ecosystem in the United States, it quickly becomes obvious that the omission of smaller newspapers is fundamentally flawed. In fact, Reader (2018) noted that "almost 98 percent [of U.S. newspapers] had circulations below 50,000, about 84 percent of all newspapers were "non-dailies/weeklies," and about three-fourths of total print circulation was in the "community newspaper" sector (weeklies and dailies under 50,000 circulation)" (p. 33).

One reason that smaller news organizations often get ignored when the news industry is discussed undoubtedly concerns how hard it is to define what makes a news organization "local," or "community" or "rural," or some other similar categorization (Lauterer, 2006). While these terms are often used interchangeably, they, in fact, mean very different things. Rural news is its own thing, with its own mission and its own role in society (Corbett, 1992). The other reason why these organization regularly get ignored, particularly in academic research, is the static nature of their organizations; there is very little change at these types of places over the decades, very little of the innovation that scholars often want to study. In journalism, innovation usually occurs only after years of fighting it, only when the demand to adapt from audiences or economics becomes impossible to ignore. For journalism, an industry married to norms and ethics, innovation is often significantly difficult. This is especially the case for rural news organizations.

Defining Rural News

When we say rural news, there is no consensual definition from practitioners or journalism studies scholars. Typically, the rural weekly newspapers that make up the largest portion of rural news organizations in the United States are classified as either local news or community news (Hess, 2013). For a news organization to truly be considered a purveyor of local news, the

DOI: 10.4324/9781003414582-2

outlet must provide its audience “along with primary news values, a sense of community and localness” that shapes the published material (Hess & Waller, 2012, p. 169). This is an important attribute, as too often scholarship lumps all news produced under any geographic moniker as local. For example, in their important critique of the problems inherent in the content produced by many larger metropolitan newspapers, Usher (2021) considers such sizable organizations as, say, the *Boston Globe* as local news. While a newspaper such as the *Globe* does, yes, publish news primarily local to Massachusetts and parts of New Hampshire or Rhode Island, it is not an outlet providing any “sense of community and localness.” It is a monolithic metropolitan newspaper not at all immune to the enormous economic disruptions impacting journalism writ large, but absolutely not encountering the bleak outlook facing many truly local news outlets. A billionaire owner can purchase an entity such as the *Boston Globe*, change some processes, and put it on a path toward economic prosperity at best, sound financial footing at least (Kennedy, 2018). But for true local news of the kind that Hess (2013) and this book discuss, “fixing local news in the United States necessitates more than simply an organization-by-organization approach” that comes from a billionaire owner making some tweaks, but rather a complete revitalization of the economics of the entire local news ecosystem (Ferrucci & Perreault 2022, p. 2).

While local journalism can be defined broadly with, as previously mentioned, an entity that covers more than an entire state, community journalism is far more connected to a smaller, specific geographic place (Reader & Hatcher, 2011). In fact, when considering that definition of local journalism, many of the organizations that would fall under the categorization are now, in the digital age, local in name only with national or even global corporations owning them and many of the controlling decision-makers based in offices far away from the newsroom (Franklin, 2006). While a broad characterization of community journalism might simply describe it as “journalism as practiced by weeklies and small dailies with intensely local focus” (Lauterer, 2006, p. xviii), that definition is still broad and does not differentiate the concept beyond noting a concentrated local angle. More specifically, community journalism focuses first “on information connected to everyday life, and second, its media members tend to develop a closer, more intimate connection to the community they serve” (Meyer & Speakman, 2019, para. 3). That more nuanced description brings together various historical strands of journalism studies research to better situate community journalism as less of a traditional watchdog of power, but more in the role of a populist mobilizer, a form of media that strengthens community ties and is predicated on deeper connection between journalist and audience. For many, community journalism is a form of media that produces a type of activism on behalf of the public interest of its audience, a category of journalism less beholden to industry norms in the pursuit of civic engagement and self-government for community citizens (Altschull, 1996). In the United States, most true community journalism outlets are still owned and operated within the geographic community (Finneman, Ferrucci, & Mathews, 2023).

To Lowrey, Brozana, and Mackay (2008, p. 293), community journalism is a distinct entity, a particular type of media that informs a specific local community "about itself and engage[s] in a search for meaning and sense making. Similarly, community journalism … encourages the pursuit of, and negotiation about, the meaning of shared symbols, such as resources, issues, and institutions." Together, these definitions illustrate what separates community journalism from the more general concept of local journalism: While both are definitively connected to a physical geographic location, even if audiences are no longer necessarily located in those geographic spaces, community journalism embraces a multitude of functions that include not only disseminating important information necessary for self-government, but also boosterism, sensemaking, and, perhaps most vitally, the function of discursively producing a shared understanding of community for members. It is important to note that while community journalism far more often does not produce the type of investigative journalism often correlated with holding powerful people accountable and is more often connected to bolstering community ties through boosterism, it still does occasionally perform accountability functions. In fact, through community journalism, the creation of community solidarity becomes an essential driver to citizens in terms of their notions of what defines important news (Wahl-Jorgensen, 2022). In effect, community journalism often embodies far more functions than what could be constituted as local news. What separates community from simply local news is the "intimacy that the organizations and the people who practice (community journalism) share with the institutions and individuals they cover" (Rosenberry, 2011, p. 25). This multitude of purposes is even more prevalent in news weeklies, the kind of non-daily newspapers often found in rural areas of the United States. These news weeklies are vital disseminators of community journalism, the type of news outlets that often have no other competition when it comes to producing local news within the geographic communities in which they exist.

Disruptions of Local News

In examining the entirety of local news, numerous disruptions facing the field become apparent. Many of the outlets making up this ecosystem face continuous calls to innovate, a vague and directionless refrain that intentionally or, at least, recklessly disregards the economic constraints facing these organizations. Today, for local news, "there is now an accepted mantra: become digital or die," an order that does not account for numerous obstacles many local news organizations would encounter during the process of digitization (Hess & Waller, 2020, p. 60). The reality is that many local news organizations are so embedded in their communities, providing that aforementioned sense of place, that any kind of digital innovation or change in historical news production processes could result in a detrimental effect to public participation or robust overall civic engagement (Lewis, Kaufhold, & Lasorsa, 2010). These local newspapers, it must be acknowledged, are the catalyst for civic engagement, as other forms of news organizations simply do not have the same impact. At least historically, research suggests that citizens' ties to various community institutions is only correlated to one type of news consumption: local newspapers (Viswanath et al., 1990). Many true local news organizations understand their role in the community. These newspapers, the most prominent deliverer of local news, comprehend that any risk taken, such as the one that comes along with digitization, necessitates the economic capital that could make the organization even more precarious. This is potentially disastrous for a local community, as "when a newspaper is lost, there are impacts on everything from engagement with politics to access to public health information, with particular demographics, such as the elderly, impacted differentially" (Muurlink and Marx 2023, p. 9).

The main issue facing all forms of local news, though, is that in a pre-internet time, citizens accessed local news geographically, and this remained one of the only ways for people to maintain a sense of place by receiving information about the geographic area. But in the digital age, this is no longer the case as "digital news environments shift from spaces that audiences move through and around into places of meaning and significance" (Gutsche & Hess, 2020, p. 587). Moreover, what this means is that no longer does physical space hold an almost monopoly on a feeling of place, and that people can now attain that same feeling through platforms such as social media (Toff & Mathews, 2021). However, even in a digital environment, local news "plays an important role in constructing the idea of 'community' or collectivity" (Hess & Waller, 2014, p. 131). Today, while the concept of local news can be considered something without much utility since geographic space exudes less agency over the sense of place, the need for robust community journalism remains of significant importance (Figure 2.1).

Understanding the Rural News Weekly

As illustrated, local and, more specifically, community news provides an essential function within geographic or, as Hess (2013) described it, geosocial spaces, a function that serves an unambiguously foundational role in undergirding democracy. As previously noted, local and community news can come in many forms, and while most community news is produced within the broad confines of what would be considered a newspaper, rural areas in the United States rely almost solely on rural news weeklies, hyperlocal newspapers often published once a week (Abernathy, 2018). These news weeklies are often part of the fabric of a community, showcasing the cultural ideals of these areas or, as Rogers (1942) contended almost a century ago, a rural news weekly "usually presents a folksy democracy" (p. 151). The idea is that a rural news weekly's content often reflects the values and priorities of the place where it

Vol. 7: No. 33 | Thursday, March 31, 2022 | www.harveycountynow.com | Newton, KS | $1.25

Newton Board reviews plan to pare $900K from budget

BY BLAKE SPURNEY
HARVEY COUNTY NOW STAFF

NEWTON—Newton Superintendent Fred Van Ranken told the USD-373 Board of Education on Monday night that no superintendent liked having the conversation he was about to have with board members.

Van Ranken outlined plans for trying to fill a revenue shortfall caused by declining enrollment. The looming deficit primarily is caused by a declining student enrollment brought about by the COVID-19 pandemic. Van Ranken showed a graph that listed Newton's peak enrollment of 3,770 students in 2011-12. That number has dropped to 3,277 during the current year, and the district's projections have it falling to fewer than 2,900 by 2026-27.

"I didn't come here to cut budgets," Van Ranken said. "I came here to build a great learning environment for kids."

Budget cuts are necessary because the district receives its allotment of state funding based on enrollment. Van Ranken said 60.5 percent of the district's budgets went to salaries. He said he had been through three budget cuts since 2000. He said the district couldn't use federal Elementary and Secondary

See BUDGET / A8

Newton High School grad brings racecar to school

WENDY NUGENT/HARVEY COUNTY NOW

Newton High School student Adrianna Alvarez enjoys herself sitting in Kyle Wiens's, right, racing car recently during the Newton High School experiential learning day, where people in a variety of professions spoke to students. "It was fun," Alvarez said about being in the vehicle. "I had never been on one."

The need for speed

BY WENDY NUGENT
HARVEY COUNTY NOW STAFF

NEWTON—Police probably have been concerned with drag-racing teens with every generation since the Industrial Revolution. However, even though there was a racecar parked in front of Newton High School (NHS) recently, no police were around. They didn't seem much concerned.

That's because an adult brought it there as part of the school's experiential learning day. Kyle Wiens, a 2012 NHS grad, brought what he called a "dirt modified" car, which he also referred to as "dirt oval," since they drive in circles.

"I've been racing it five or so years after the one I had before I had that," Wiens said to one of the classes that went out in the cold to see the car and listen to Wiens.

He told students that to pay for his first car, he got a job at Dillons and worked all summer. Wiens also said they've had good sponsor support and that they go to Mel Hambleton Ford and spend $1,500 on tires alone as

See RACECAR / A16

Taxi rate increase makes getting around difficult for low-income Newton residents

BY WENDY NUGENT
HARVEY COUNTY NOW STAFF

NEWTON—An increase in the cost of public transportation has made it harder for those with low incomes or who are disabled to get around.

Fees for OT Cab Company increased from $7.50 to $12 in March, according to information discussed at a recent county commission meeting. The cab service is the only reliable form of public transportation in the county outside of Harvey County InterUrban.

InterUrban is only available to people who need mobility devices that are medically required.

Harvey County does subsidize taxi rides for lower-income people with a cab discount card, according to Lona Kelly, Harvey County Department on Aging director.

People 185 percent below the federal poverty level and not on Medicare or KanCare in Kansas are eligible, Kelly said.

"That's been going on for a long time," she said. "Since 2012, the [OT Cab] rates have pretty much been set."

She said the local cab company had a private discount, which was $1.50, and continued

See TAXI / A8

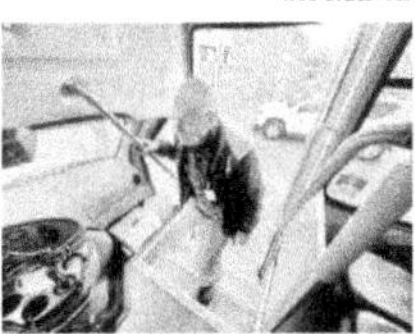

WENDY NUGENT/HARVEY COUNTY NOW

Ken Frey, a Harvey InterUrban bus driver, prepares to start a shift with the bus on Monday afternoon. Harvey InterUrban and OT Cab are the majority of, if not the

Figure 2.1 *Harvey County Now* has a weekly circulation of about 4,000 and is based in Newton, Kansas, a community of about 20,000 people near Wichita. Joey Young launched the newspaper in 2015 as a competitor to the then GateHouse-owned *Newton Kansan* to provide a locally owned alternative. The newspaper is an example of a rural news weekly that takes pride in the service it provides to its community. Courtesy of Kansas Publishing Ventures.

is published. The "reporting reflects a community's characteristics and concerns and reinforces the existing social order" (Corbett, 1992, p. 936). In a sense, while journalism might often be regarded as a watchdog of power, in rural communities it often serves a foundation for many of the hegemonic notions that implicitly diffuse across a community. In a case study of a rural news weekly in Colorado, an area that became a news desert when a nearby corporate newspaper shuttered, Ferrucci and Alaimo (2020) illustrated how even a brand-new nonprofit news organization matured into a news entity that "strengthens the overall ties of a community, which is a fundamental tenant of a strong democracy" (p. 502). Fundamentally, even though this new rural news weekly took on a more innovative market model as a nonprofit with a diversity of revenue streams, its essential function mirrored historical rural news weeklies. While it of course disseminated important information to citizens, its most prominent role in the community was to uphold community ideals and strengthen ties between community stakeholders. These ties created a strong relationship between a rural news weekly and its community, as "for much of the 20th century, small-town weekly newspapers connected with more small towns and villages on a regular basis" than any other type of media (Garfrerick, 2010, p. 153). While social media platforms might provide some of this connection now in ways rural news weeklies cannot (Toff & Mathews 2021), these news organizations continue performing this role into the first decades of the 21st century (Smith, 2015). There are, however, potential negatives to this main role of rural news weeklies. If an organization primarily conceives its role as a strengthener of community, "this decision can be seen as shielding the residents from the controversy and preventing any psychological harm" (Mathews, 2021, p. 681–682). However, this does not mean rural news weeklies avoid holding power accountable (e.g., Corbett, 1992), but rather that sometimes a news weekly's roles of providing accountability journalism and strengthening community bonds can clash. It is important to realize, though, that all news organizations embody unique functions, and the rural news weekly is no different (Rogers, 1942).

Disruptive Innovation

Due to this long-standing and quite resilient role within communities, rural news weeklies are often considered anti-innovation or unchanging. Many of these rural news weeklies are not owned by chains but remain led by local ownership. This limits their ability to "maximize the amount of content they post, which in turn may impact the prominence given to their content in news feeds," which results in not being able to optimize social media usage (Toff & Mathews, 2021, p. 13). These difficulties inherent in change are, however, not simply confined to digital technologies at rural news organizations.

The most salient issue with industry change agents – or, as Hepp and Loosen (2022) dub them, pioneer journalists – comes in the form of organizational makeup. Journalism to both professionals and academics alike is a public service that innovates only to further its mission (Gynnild, 2014). Therefore, despite an obvious codependent relationship between journalism and technology, innovation is not something often easily successful within the field (Mari, 2019). In most industries, furthermore, innovation is not a given because a "mastery of old technology does not imply a mastery of the new" (Anderson & Tushman, 1991, p. 28). In journalism, innovation usually occurs only after years of fighting it, only when the demand to adapt from audiences or economics becomes impossible to ignore. However, for journalism, an industry married to norms and ethics, innovation is often significantly more difficult (Barrett et al., 2015; Stinchcombe, 1965).

To better explicate how industries and organizations adapt when implementing disruptive technologies, Christensen (2003) developed the theory of disruptive innovation, which contends that market forces strongly influence innovation, but that historical or more stable fields struggle to adapt. When an industry operates in a similar manner for extended time periods, those practices become an essential part of the job, which means those industries are typically not nimble enough to adapt seamlessly (Christensen, 2013; King & Baatartogtokh, 2015). This is especially relevant for rural news organizations, ones with minimal staff that already do more than counterparts at large metropolitan news. These low-populated newsrooms work in a specific way, meaning any change catalyzes significant butterfly effects. Before Christensen's theory, scholars labeled this issue the liability of newness. This concept asserts that when faced with new disruptive technological implementation, old organizations must essentially become new ones in basically all manners (Stinchcombe, 1965). For rural news organizations that have worked the same way for a century and are now tasked with innovation, employees are not necessarily adept at accomplishing new tasks (Ferrucci & Perreault, 2021).

It is difficult for rural news weeklies to innovate in ways associated with technology or in manners that require larger financial investments and other resources often not available to smaller organizations (Ferrucci & Perreault, 2021). But their role as a community builder and strengthener provide a framework for less discussed innovation. In a sense, "because of the inherently localized nature of the community weekly, the accepted standards of professional journalism do not apply in full to community weeklies" (Garfrerick, 2010, p. 151). What this means is, because of their unique role performed within communities, rural news weeklies can alter processes or practices in a way that may not completely align with industry normative processes, something not possible at larger organizations. This became visible during the COVID-19 pandemic when weekly newspaper journalists became more "nimble in adapting their ordinary reporting routines to extraordinary conditions" (Finneman & Thomas 2021, p. 341). All of these characteristics and functions make rural news organizations essential elements of their communities (Ferrucci et al., 2023).

The Urgency of a New Model

Rural news weeklies, overwhelmingly, deliver the essential function of "covering small towns and the rural countryside around them" (Rosenberry, 2011, p. 37). Therefore, the loss of these local institutions can significantly and negatively affect the communities. The "newspaper death rate," or the number of newspapers that go out of business in the United States, has increased since the early years of the 21st century. It now averages more than "10 a month, with a particular spike after the 2008 Great Recession" (Stites, 2018). In fact, experts believe that, in the United States, by the year 2025, "one-third of American newspapers that existed roughly two decades ago will be out of business" (Sullivan, 2022). Researcher Penny Abernathy (2018) dubbed the areas where local news no longer exists news deserts. Specifically, "the most hard-hit segment of news organizations is unequivocally local news" (Ferrucci & Rossi 2022, p. 4096). Many expected new digital news organizations "to come riding to the rescue of community journalism," but this did not occur, and many rural areas of the country remain news deserts (Stites, 2018). Moreover, the vast majority of newer news organizations are not in rural areas (Matherly & Greenwood, 2021; Miller, 2018).

When a community becomes a news desert, the deficiency of news "poses a far-reaching danger to civic engagement, the accountability of government, and, many analysts argue, democracy itself" (Miller, 2018, p. 59). In short, when an area becomes a news desert after, for example, a rural news weekly closes, Matherly and Greenwood (2021) found corruption flourishes within those communities. In a sense, the existence of news deserts compounds already information-precarious areas of the United States. When a rural area loses its existing news source, that source typically represents almost 100% of the original reporting about that community (Miller, 2018). Across the country, this leaves many non-metropolitan areas of the world without any news coverage whatsoever (Örnebring, 2018; Ferrucci et al., 2023). Beyond information, accountability, and democratic ideals, the existence of a news desert also destabilizes community ties as local news organizations often play a vital community-building role within rural areas and small towns (Mathews, 2021). This is, as previously noted, especially salient for rural news weeklies, the kind of news organization that often operates in isolation in these geographic areas, regularly providing the only professional source of local news to their communities. Without rural news weeklies, those areas become places with little accountability, fewer social ties, and a lack of that folksy democracy that Rogers (1942) discussed or the local boosterism described by Robinson (2014). With this community journalism and, particularly rural news weeklies, under significant financial duress for more than a decade (Remez, 2012), the losses potentially facing rural areas are immense. It has become essential that these community organizations find a more economically stable operating model.

References

Abernathy, P. M. (2018). The expanding news desert. University of North Carolina. https://www.cislm.org/wp-content/uploads/2018/10/The-Expanding-News-Desert-10_14-Web.pdf

Altschull, J. H. (1996). A crisis of conscience: Is community journalism the answer? *Journal of Mass Media Ethics*, *11*(3), 166–172.

Anderson, P., & Tushman, M. L. (1991). Managing through cycles of technological change. *Research-Technology Management*, *34*(3), 26–31.

Barrett, M., Davidson, E., Prabhu, J., & Vargo, S. L. (2015). Service innovation in the digital age: Key contributions and future directions. *MIS Quarterly*, *39*(1), 135–154.

Christensen, C. M. (2003). *The innovator's solution: Creating and sustaining successful growth*. Harvard Business Press.

Christensen, C. M. (2013). *The innovator's dilemma: When new technologies cause great firms to fail*. Harvard Business Review Press.

Corbett, J. B. (1992). Rural and urban newspaper coverage of wildlife: Conflict, community and bureaucracy. *Journalism Quarterly*, *69*(4), 929–937.

Ferrucci, P., & Alaimo, K. I. (2020). Escaping the news desert: Nonprofit news and open-system journalism organizations. *Journalism*, *21*(4), 489–506.

Ferrucci, P., Finneman, T., Heckman, M., & Walck, P. E. (2023). A discursive evolution: Trade publications explain news deserts to United States journalists. *Media and Communication*, *11*(3), 1–10.

Ferrucci, P., & Perreault, G. (2021). The liability of newness: Journalism, innovation and the issue of core competencies. *Journalism Studies*, *22*(11), 1436–1449.

Ferrucci, P., & Perreault, G. (2022). Local is now national: The athletic as a model for online local news. *New Media & Society*. https://doi.org/10.1177%2F14614448221117748

Ferrucci, P., & Rossi, M. (2022). "Pivoting to instability": Metajournalistic discourse, reflexivity and the economics and effects of a shrinking industry. *International Journal of Communication*, *16*(2022), 4095–4114.

Finneman, T., Ferrucci, P., & Mathews, N. (2023). Revenue & readership: Rescuing & reviving rural journalism. *Journalism Practice*, 1–19.

Finneman, T., & Thomas, R. J. (2021). "You had to be reporting constantly": COVID-19's impact on US weekly newspapers' journalistic routines. *Newspaper Research Journal*, *42*(3), 330–345.

Franklin, B. (2006). *Local journalism and local media: Making the local news*. Routledge.

Garfrerick, B. H. (2010). The community weekly newspaper: Telling America's stories. *American Journalism*, *27*(3), 151–157.

Gutsche, J., Robert E, & Hess, K. (2020). Placeification: The transformation of digital news spaces into "places" of meaning. *Digital Journalism*, *8*(5), 586–595.

Gynnild, A. (2014). Journalism innovation leads to innovation journalism: The impact of computational exploration on changing mindsets. *Journalism*, *15*(6), 713–730.

Hepp, A., & Loosen, W. (2022). Beyond innovation: Pioneer journalism and the refiguration of journalism. In P. Ferrucci & S. A. Eldridge II (Eds.), *The institutions changing journalism* (pp. 118–135). Routledge.

Hess, K. (2013). Breaking boundaries: Recasting the "local" newspaper as "geo-social" news in a digital landscape. *Digital Journalism*, *1*(1), 48–63.

Hess, K., & Waller, L. (2012). 'The snowtown we know and love': Small newspapers and heinous crimes. *Rural Society, 21*(2), 116–125.

Hess, K., & Waller, L. (2014). Geo-social journalism: Reorienting the study of small commercial newspapers in a digital environment. *Journalism Practice, 8*(2), 121–136.

Hess, K., & Waller, L. (2020). Charting the media innovations landscape for regional and rural newspapers. *Australian Journalism Review, 42*(1), 59–75.

Kennedy, D. (2018). *The return of the Moguls: How Jeff Bezos and John Henry are remaking newspapers for the twenty-first century*. University Press of New England.

King, A. A., & Baatartogtokh, B. (2015). How useful is the theory of disruptive innovation? *MIT Sloan Management Review, 57*(1), 77.

Lauterer, J. (2006). *Community journalism: Relentlessly local*. University of North Carolina Press.

Lewis, S. C., Kaufhold, K., & Lasorsa, D. L. (2010). Thinking about citizen journalism: The philosophical and practical challenges of user-generated content for community newspapers. *Journalism Practice, 4*(2), 163–179.

Lowrey, W., Brozana, A., & Mackay, J. B. (2008). Toward a measure of community journalism. *Mass Communication and Society, 11*(3), 275–299.

Mari, W. (2019). *A short history of disruptive journalism technologies: 1960–1990*. Routledge.

Matherly, T., & Greenwood, B. N. (2021). No news is bad news: Political corruption, news deserts, and the decline of the fourth estate. *Academy of Management Proceedings*. https://doi.org/10.5465/AMBPP.2021.10153abstract

Mathews, N. (2021). The community caretaker role: How weekly newspapers shielded their communities while covering the Mississippi ICE raids. *Journalism Studies, 22*(5), 670–687.

Meyer, H., & Speakman, B. (2019). Community journalism. *Oxford Research encyclopedia of communication*. Oxford University Press. https://doi-org.ezproxy.uio.no/10.1093/acrefore/9780190228613.013.789.

Miller, J. (2018). News deserts: No news is bad news. *Urban Policy, 2018*, 59–76.

Muurlink, O., & Marx, E. V. (2023). Out of print: What the pandemic-era newspaper crisis in Australia teaches us about the role of rural and regional newspapers in creating sustainable communities. *Sustainability, 15*(6), 1–12.

Örnebring, H. (2018). Journalism cannot solve journalism's problems. *Journalism, 20*(1), 1–3. https://journals.sagepub.com/doi/10.1177/1464884918808690

Reader, B. (2018). Despite losses, community newspapers still dominate the U.S. market. *Newspaper Research Journal, 39*(1): 32–41. doi:10.1177/0739532918765467.

Reader, B., & Hatcher, J. A. (2011). *Foundations of community journalism*. Sage Publications.

Remez, M. (2012). How community news is faring. *State of the News Media*. Pew Research Center.

Robinson, S. (2014). Introduction. *Community journalism midst media revolution* (1st ed., pp. 113–120). Taylor & Francis.

Rogers, C. E. (1942). The role of the weekly newspaper. *The Annals of the American Academy of Political and Social Science, 219*(1), 151–157.

Rosenberry, J. (2011). Key works: Some connections between journalism and community. In B. Reader & J. A. Hatcher (Eds.), *Foundations of community journalism* (pp. 25–42). Sage Publications.

Smith, C. C. (2015). *Weekly newspapering: Iowa's small-town newspapers, their news workers, and their community roles*. The University of Iowa.

Stinchcombe, A. L. (1965). Social structure and organizations. In J. March (Ed.), *Handbook of organizations* (pp. 153–193). Rand McNally.

Stites, T. (2018). About 1,300 U.S. communities have totally lost news coverage, UNC news desert study finds. *Poynter*. https://www.poynter.org/news/about-1300-us-communities-have-totally-lost-news-coverage-unc-news-desert-study-finds

Sullivan, M. (2022). Every week, two more newspapers close – and 'news deserts' grow larger. *The Washington Post*. https://www.washingtonpost.com/media/2022/06/29/news-deserts-newspapers-democracy/

Toff, B., & Mathews, N. (2021). Is social media killing local news? An examination of engagement and ownership patterns in US community news on Facebook. *Digital Journalism*, 1–20.

Usher, N. (2021). *News for the rich, white, and blue: How place and power distort American journalism*. Columbia University Press.

Viswanath, K., Finnegan, J. R., Jr, Rooney, B., Jr, & Potter, J., Jr (1990). Community ties in a rural midwest community and use of newspapers and cable television. *Journalism Quarterly*, *67*(4), 899–911.

Wahl-Jorgensen, K. (2022). Community journalism as responsible journalism. In J. Lynch & C. Rice (Eds.), *Responsible journalism in conflicted societies* (pp. 30–43). Routledge.

3 Publishers

Stuck in the Status Quo

Nick Mathews

A Kansas publisher, still shy of her 40s yet seasoned in the news industry, finds herself deeply drawn to the boundless possibilities of diversifying revenue avenues, unlocking novel sources of income and, ultimately, fortifying her organization's financial future. Fueled by an insatiable thirst for knowledge, she devours industry podcasts, participates in state conventions, and consumes copious content on newsroom economics and groundbreaking practices. Her intrigue for industry innovation seemingly knows no bounds. Yet it is accompanied by an overwhelming sense of paralysis, preventing action.

She expresses both admiration and intimidation toward hosting an event like Blues, Brews & Barbecue, an annual music and food festival in Kansas organized by Joey and Lindsey Young and *Harvey County Now.* "It amazes me that they do that," she said. "It scares me. It would scare me to death to try that here. But, I mean, it seems to be very successful for them." Likewise, she is intrigued by the concept of a news organization owner embracing a pay-what-you-think-it's-worth membership approach, rather than a traditional set subscription fee. "It made me think," she said, "but I'm not ready to jump on that ledge yet." While curious about exploring events, memberships, e-newsletters, and other prospects, she grapples with the practicalities of implementation. "I would say that I would be concerned with staff members," she said. "Expanding on what we're already doing is hard. Because there's not enough time, and we're already stretched thin."

Despite interest in innovation, her concentration is on tradition. "We have to focus on our print product. We can't just switch it to something else or take away from it to do other things," she said. "So that's where it's hard. I think we have to adapt every day. We have to continue to adapt, or we won't survive. But change is hard, always." The Kansas publisher is not alone in this status quo state, stuck in the day-to-day and week-to-week decision-making, unable to move forward. She can find solace in the company of other rural, weekly newsroom publishers across the country. In this chapter, we argue there is a pervasive trend within their ranks: Their overwhelming choice of action is a resolute commitment to inaction.

DOI: 10.4324/9781003414582-3

This chapter's findings are grounded in two data sets – a survey of 100+ rural, weekly newspaper leaders and focus groups with 19 newsroom leaders from North Dakota, South Dakota, Kansas, and Nebraska. In the aggregate, the survey data find leaders do not demonstrate a willingness to contemplate making business changes to diversify their revenue streams. Their focus predominantly centers around selling public services already conducted in-house at the newspaper (such as commercial printing), which have been long-standing practices nationwide. The survey data illustrates an overall hesitancy to embrace contemporary innovations, reflecting a general reluctance to explore new approaches and, as a result, perpetuating the prevailing status quo. The focus groups deliver valuable nuances to the aggregate survey findings, revealing three distinct yet interconnected tensions that illuminate the underlying reasons for the collective standstill. First, there is an overarching tension between tradition and innovation, signifying a struggle between short-term pressures and long-term planning. Second, tension arises from resource constraints and staffing limitations that directly impede their capacity to contemplate innovation. Third, there is tension as leaders display apprehension when considering options – especially donations – to attain financial stability. Concerns about compromising editorial independence or jeopardizing their standing within the community loom over their willingness to explore other options.

Overall, this chapter's mixed-methods approach finds rural, weekly newspapers leaders cling to their traditional strengths, especially the print product and current revenue model, fueled in part by the fear of losing loyal readers and advertisers. While the leaders acknowledge change is constant – whether they choose the change or it is forced upon them – their actions are limited. Seemingly preferring resting on their laurels to the perils of the future, the leaders linger in the interim, biding their time and anticipating the emergence of an industry trailblazer. In other words, many newsroom leaders would rather follow than lead into the future.

The Survey

Before we created a business model to experiment, we deployed surveys to weekly newspaper publishers and rural residents to better understand their attitudes toward funding local news. In this chapter, we analyze the publisher data. In Chapter 4, we analyze the reader data.

Using both academic literature and industry trade magazine publications on the subject, we created a list of 16 possible funding options that included strategies that weekly publishers currently use, as well as well-publicized newer strategies. Publishers were told to check all of the options they would be willing to consider. Strategies included office supplies, print subscriptions, graphic design services, commercial printing, e-newsletters, memberships, marketing

Table 3.1 The ages of publishers per state who filled out the survey.

	Kansas	*Nebraska*	*North Dakota*	*South Dakota*	*Total*
20–30	0	3 (10%)	0	1 (4.5%)	4 (3.8%)
31–40	5 (13.9%)	6 (20%)	1 (5.9%)	2 (9.1%)	14 (13.3%)
41–50	5 (13.9%)	7 (23.3%)	2 (11.8%)	2 (9.1%)	16 (15.2%)
51–60	9 (25%)	6 (20%)	8 (47.1%)	10 (45.5%)	33 (31.4%)
61–70	12 (33.3%)	5 (16.7%)	4 (23.5%)	6 (27.3%)	27 (25.7%)
71+	5 (13.9%)	3 (10%)	2 (11.8%)	1 (4.5%)	11 (10.5%)
Total	36 (34.3%)	30 (28.6%)	17 (16.2)	22 (21%)	105

services, legal notices, grants, government support, foundations/large donors, events, donations, digital subscriptions, and advertising. The survey also collected demographic information about the publisher and their news organizations (e.g., age, gender, geographic location).

We asked two project partners – the South Dakota Newspaper Association and the Kansas Press Association – to share the survey with other state newspaper associations across the nation and encourage them to pass it along to their newspaper-owner members to fill out. As an incentive for participation, those who included an email address at the end of the survey were entered in drawings for ten Amazon gift cards worth $100 each. The researchers opened the survey in December 2021 and January 2022, and then emailed several reminders for state newspaper associations to ask their members to complete it. Due to higher participation in Great Plains states (North Dakota, South Dakota, Nebraska, and Kansas), we narrowed our scope of analysis to this geographic area.

Overall, the survey generated 106 results (although some participants chose not to answer some demographic questions): 17 from North Dakota, 22 from South Dakota, 30 from Nebraska, and 37 from Kansas. The 106 participants owned a total of 176 newspapers. The majority of responding publishers' newspapers operate in towns with fewer than 5,000 people (88.1%). Furthermore, 51% of respondents were female. Broken down by age, 17.1% were under age 40, 46.6% were 41–60, and 36.2% were 61 or older, with Table 3.1 providing a state breakdown and Table 3.2 providing a gender breakdown. Table 3.3 illustrates the population sizes served by these publishers.

Table 3.2 The gender of publishers per state who filled out the survey.

	Kansas	*Nebraska*	*North Dakota*	*South Dakota*	*Total*
Female	18 (50%)	15 (50%)	9 (56.3%)	11 (50%)	53 (51%)
Male	18 (50%)	15 (50%)	7 (43.8%)	11 (50%)	51 (49%)
Non-binary	0	0	0	0	0
Total	36	30	16	22	104

Table 3.3 The population sizes of the communities served by these newspaper publishers. Some respondents own multiple newspapers and filled out the survey for each one.

	Kansas	*Nebraska*	*North Dakota*	*South Dakota*	*Total*
Under 1,000	5 (9.4%)	20 (42.6%)	19 (48.7%)	18 (48.6%)	62 (35.2%)
1,001–3,000	27 (50.9%)	16 (34%)	18 (46.2%)	10 (27%)	71 (40.3%)
3,001–5,000	9 (17%)	7 (14.9%)	2 (5.1%)	4 (10.8%)	22 (12.5%)
5,001–7,000	4 (7.5%)	2 (4.3%)	0	0	6 (3.4%)
7,001–10,000	2 (3.8%)	2 (4.3%)	0	1 (2.7%)	5 (2.8%)
More than 10,000	6 (11.3%)	0	0	4 (10.8%)	10 (5.7%)
Total	53	47	39	37	176

The survey asked publishers for general demographic information about their newspapers. The majority of newspapers have a website (84.9%), have an e-edition (76.7%), and publish weekly (95.3%).

Regardless of tax-filing status, news organizations can utilize multiple revenue streams. Of the publishers who answered a question about taxation status, 97% operated for-profit newspapers. Only three nonprofit newspapers were included in the surveyed publishers across the four states. The publishers surveyed also oversee newspapers that overwhelmingly (97%) publish print editions; therefore, few oversee digitally native news organizations. Fundamentally, the publishers surveyed manage news organizations that resemble the financial model of news popularized and fossilized in the late 19th century. These newspapers rely primarily on advertising and subscriptions for revenue, with Table 3.4 breaking down all of their financial methods.

The majority of newspapers represented in the survey rely on traditional, historical funding streams. However, unlike the more mainstream relatively new funding streams employed by metropolitan U.S. news organizations – such as membership models, foundation grants, or crowdfunding – rural news organizations rely on revenue from activities such as graphic design services (39.2%), commercial printing services (48.1%), or office supply sales (20.4%). This illustrates how these newspapers are willing to think broadly about diversifying revenue streams, but these activities revolve around selling services already conducted in-house at the newspaper. Furthermore, these are strategies that weeklies in Great Plains states have used for decades, with the data as a whole illustrating a reluctance to try contemporary innovation.

The survey also asked newspaper publishers which revenue streams they perceived as viable in their communities, as illustrated in Table 3.5. Unsurprisingly, the majority believed advertising, subscriptions, and legal notices remained the most viable revenue streams, thereby enforcing journalism's struggle to adapt. Meaningfully, though, while 100% of newspapers rely on advertising currently, only 85.1% of those believe that advertising is viable, signifying a tacit acknowledgment of dwindling revenue from advertising.

Table 3.4 These are the revenue streams currently used by the publishers who completed the survey. Publishers who owned multiple newspapers filled out the survey for each one.

Revenue stream	*Number of newspapers*
Advertising	181 (100%)
Print subscriptions	175 (96.7%)
Legal notices	158 (87.3%)
Digital subscriptions	135 (74.6%)
Commercial printing services	87 (48.1%)
Graphic design services	71 (39.2%)
Office supply sales	37 (20.4%)
Marketing services	32 (17.7%)
Donations	24 (13.3%)
Events	23 (12.7%)
Newsletters	23 (12.7%)
Grants	14 (7.7%)
Government support (beyond PPP)	7 (3.9%)
Foundations/large donors	2 (1.1%)
Membership	2 (1.1%)
Custom apparel services	2 (1.1%)
Pagination services	1 (.6%)
Social media consulting	1 (.6%)

Table 3.5 The revenue streams perceived as viable by the publishers who took the survey. Publishers who owned multiple newspapers filled out the survey for each one.

Revenue stream	*Number of newspapers*
Advertising	154 (85.1%)
Print subscriptions	150 (82.9%)
Digital subscriptions	134 (74%)
Legal notices	128 (70.7%)
Graphic design services	89 (49.2%)
Commercial printing services	87 (48.1%)
Marketing services	86 (47.5%)
Donations	76 (42%)
Events	74 (40.9%)
Newsletters	67 (37%)
Grants	66 (36.5%)
Foundations/large donors	63 (34.8%)
Government support (beyond PPP)	61 (33.7%)
Office supply sales	61 (33.7%)
Membership	57 (31.5)

Also of note is that these publishers perceive graphic design, commercial printing, and marketing as more viable than revenue streams used in metro journalism, such as events, newsletters, and foundation grants. Fundamentally, it seems, rural publishers do not believe revenue streams that rely on journalism already happening – membership, newsletters, grants — are nearly as viable as ones that involve added services to the community.

While understanding that what survey participants say they would support and what they would actually support could be different, the results suggest an unwillingness to enact mechanisms to diversify revenue streams. It would seem like publishers are leaving money on the table and not maximizing potential economic viability.

Tradition versus Innovation

The overarching tension that emerged during focus groups with newsroom owners and leaders was the classic confrontation between tradition and innovation. This clash casts a shadow on the present and future, as it juxtaposes the short-term pressures – "survival mode," as one leader described it — and long-term planning of their businesses. The immediate financial (and existential) fears the newsrooms face exert a formidable force, compelling risk aversion, stalling for the future, and undermining the mere notion of innovation.

Some leaders characterized their plight as an all-encompassing existential fight for survival. Faced with short-term pressures, particularly with escalating costs of printing and personnel, they find themselves in a ceaseless cycle of day-to-day and week-to-week decision-making. Immediate financial footing takes precedence over long-term economic prospects. "At the end of the day, it becomes a survival mode," a male North Dakota editor said, "and we will do what we have to do to survive." Facing stagnant revenues, newsroom leaders experience "an ongoing uphill slog," as a Kansas publisher described. "It takes so much energy," she said. On the other hand, some newsroom leaders conveyed a sense of contentment, bordering perilously toward complacency. They maintained no modifications were necessary for their newspapers at this time. "I'm comfortable with where I am," one Nebraska female owner said, while a female editor in the state added, "We're liking the way (the current business model) is going, so I think that's probably where we're going to stick." A dozen years into his stewardship, a South Dakota weekly owner said, "I'm pretty comfortable" with the business as it is and "I'm just going to keep doing what I'm doing for the next 12 years." Another Nebraska female owner acknowledged her intent to implement business adjustments in due course but felt comfortable with current circumstances. "I think where we're at now is probably where we're going to be with things for the next five to eight years," she said. "And I think in any business, that's as far in the future you can really look. So, right now, I am pretty comfortable." Whether cornered into survival mode or content with the status quo, these leaders see staying the course as the safe and secure decision.

During the focus groups, newsroom leaders exhibited a notable aversion to risk, a reluctance to abandon traditional business practices, and a lack of desire to peruse new revenue streams. Their concerns stem from the fear of alienating, confusing, or angering readers. One Kansas publisher recounted a poor experience with introducing change to her readers. "When we told everybody, 'We're shutting down our press, but we're printing elsewhere,' everybody thought, 'They're not printing anymore.' Some of our subscribers were confused, even though we'd run stories and everything." That experience instilled an inclination for caution when thinking about a shift from a traditional subscription model to a membership model, for example. "Because of the culture of our subscribers – they're so ingrained," she said. "And most of our subscribers are over 50. And they're just halfway paying attention to if we change something. So, if we went to a membership, I don't know if that would throw them off." Echoing the sentiment, a South Dakota publisher expressed doubts about readers' abilities to understand a new approach. "I would think that there would be a number of people who would not catch on to it," she said. "I mean, it would take a lot of explaining why we're doing this. I don't see the benefit." Similarly, a Kansas publisher was hesitant to make a change for fear of losing customers. "We can't afford to see circulation revenue drop," he said. "We need it to increase. So that's kind of where we are." A Nebraska publisher adamantly upholds traditional business and journalistic practices, stressing an aversion to "train" readers in new habits, such as reading an e-newsletter. "We have been on a trend where our circulation is going up. We're not going down," she said.

> And, at this juncture, I don't want to shift anybody more to my website than they already are. I want them buying the paper because that's where I make my money. I don't want to train them to go to a newsletter.

Ultimately, the newsroom publishers are stuck in their own state of fear or complacency, immobilized by concerns their short-term decisions will negatively impact their long-term destinies.

In lieu of considering innovations to potentially bolster their financial futures, publishers prioritize their present strengths – upholding the traditions of their print product, delivering quality local news, and banking on the enduring loyalty of readers. A female South Dakota publisher said, "The way that we're running right now seems to be pretty profitable, and we're pretty traditional, focusing on our print product. … I don't see a need to change now." A male publisher from South Dakota said, "The vast majority of my customers are print customers, and I don't think that's going to change." Approaching the end of her career, a seasoned North Dakota publisher harbors no desire to embrace sweeping, radical transformation in her operation. "I'm almost to the point now with being probably within five years of my own retirement," she said. "And I'm saying, 'OK, I'm going to start catering to the readers I have.'" Rather than venturing toward digital innovations – social media, e-newsletters, etc. – to potentially entice younger readers, she opted to add more local history content, tailored specifically to an older audience who "actually pay for the paper." A Kansas publisher remains deliberately disconnected from the "never-ending" evolution of newsroom technologies. Moreover, she dismisses the exploration of new business practices as it would detract valuable time from her primary focus. "We can't cut back on our news content. That's our bread and butter," she said. If the quality of their local news product began to waiver, she said, "I know our circulation would drop off, and I wouldn't blame them. We have to keep our focus on providing the best well-rounded coverage." Similarly, another publisher from North Dakota emphasized directing attention toward existing readership as a means of nurturing future readership. "The basics of newspapering," she said, was her news organization's fundamental focus. "Our communities support us. They see the value in us, in general. … And I think, at least here, people see it. I'm not worried about the future of newspapers here in the communities where I am." Relying on their time-tested strengths, these publishers eschew innovative changes as a strategy for their future.

Despite alarming headlines engulfing the local news landscape, publishers choose the status quo, passively listening and thinking, showcasing a pronounced lack of urgency as they await a clear, proven path to follow. This inertia persists despite unsettling realities in their communities. "Our circulation won't hold up with the current population we have over time," a female Kansas publisher acknowledged. "They're just aging out. We don't see the young subscribers to replace that. So, we're going to have to do something, I would say, in the next decade." A female North Dakota leader said. "We're doing well right now and things are fine," but added, "It's never a bad thing to look into, 'Is there a better way to do what we're doing right now?'" Furthermore, a male Kansas editor said, "I'm not under any illusion that if we just keep doing the same thing we'll be just fine." So, the news leaders do their best to keep up with the latest newsroom trends. A South Dakota news organization owner attended his state's press convention, where another weekly owner in the region discussed his rationale behind adopting an innovative membership model. "I want to see how it goes for him," the South Dakota owner said. "Maybe that means I'm not as much of a risk taker. I'm open and willing to try a new model, but, again, my jury is very much out still on it. I'm at the wait-and-see approach." Unwilling to venture into uncharted waters without clear guidance, the publishers hesitate to embrace innovative approaches. "I know I'm asking a lot to have a guarantee before I try anything," one female Kansas publisher admits, "but it would be most helpful to know what works and what doesn't."

In sum, the tension between tradition and innovation reveals the profound grip of fear on rural weekly newsrooms. Immediate financial worries, coupled with the fear that short-term decisions may endanger their long-term prospects, leave publishers in a paralyzing state of inaction and risk aversion. As they passively await a path forward, exhibiting a pronounced lack of urgency, their progress is stifled and innovation is undermined. To be sure, this silence becomes deafening amidst the cacophony of alarm bells ringing about the troubles within the local news landscape.

Resources versus Growth

At the core of the state of idleness experienced by newsroom leaders lies the tension between untapped growth possibilities and the constraints imposed by current resource limitations. While a select few newsroom leaders have managed to navigate this and implement innovative strategies for financial diversification, they remain the exception rather than the rule. In our focus groups, the majority of newsroom leaders were disheartened, if not overwhelmed, by issues of understaffing, work overload, and relentless daily demands. These challenges left them with little capacity to entertain new ideas, let alone take action to explore growth potential.

Resource limitations are a pressing concern in newsrooms around the world, but they are of particular significance in the newsrooms at the heart of this book. These rural newsrooms confront even more formidable challenges as they function with smaller staff sizes, often relying on a single individual. These constraints result in limited support, flexibility, and capacity in meeting the ever-increasing demands of the newspaper business. Furthermore, in rural areas, leaders struggle in attracting external talent, contend with a limited local employee pool, and grapple with magnified concerns of staff retention due to the scarcity of suitable replacements. Among all the topics discussed in this chapter, the issue of staffing limitations stands out as the most prominent and extensively discussed. Here, we present a curated selection of quotations that provide perspectives of newsroom leaders as they consider additional products (such as e-newsletters) or additional revenue possibilities (such as hosting events).

> *How would we expand when we think we are already stretched to the limit?
>
> – Female South Dakota publisher

> *We have such a small shop already. … We literally have all hands-on deck just to get done with a weekly newspaper. … So, it's kind of hard.
>
> – Female North Dakota publisher

> *I think it'd be tough to find the bandwidth to start (new initiatives) when most of our people are already covering a lot of different beats and wearing a lot of different hats.
>
> – Male Kansas editor

> *I am literally a one-woman newspaper, so I frankly would not have time to do something (new).
>
> – Female Nebraska publisher

> *It all goes back to staffing. If we lose a person, (a potential) newsletter is probably suspended for a few weeks until we can replace that person. That's not ideal. … I think it's a great idea, but I don't know how you resolve the staffing issue.
>
> – A second female Kansas publisher

The perceived challenges create a daunting barrier to even *consider* new ideas within their newsroom, let alone implement them. Importantly, the publishers clearly perceive new ideas as *additional* work, rather than as potential replacements for existing tasks.

During our focus groups, a few newsroom leaders stood out as contrasting voices, challenging the prevailing perception of the resources required to explore new initiatives, especially regarding e-newsletters. "We have a small staff," a South Dakota publisher explained, "so we've really streamlined how we do things." She highlighted the use of software that enables content distribution across various platforms, including their website and social media channels:

> I could see where, if you just incorporated an e-newsletter in that same thing, you know, you'd cut-and-paste your top stories to your website, cut-and-paste those top stories to your e-newsletter, cut-and-paste those top stories to your social media, and it's basically, you know, just adding one more cut-and-paste in, and I think that would work really well.

Similarly, a North Dakota publisher shared her experience of already sending out an e-newsletter with limited concerns about resources. "It's usually not a big workload," she said. Despite acknowledging the potential of software solutions to streamline the process, a Kansas publisher expressed her concerns about venturing into a newsletter:

> I would go back to staffing. It would just take time away from a different project from our newspaper to create that newsletter. Although it might be some of the same content, it would still take time to get it built together and all of that. So that would be my concern.

Newsroom leaders also highlighted concerns regarding the impact on their well-being, particularly during times of staffing transition. A Nebraska publisher shared her frustrations with constant turnover. "As soon as I train someone, they're off to bigger and better things," she said. "So, then I fall behind again because I can only do so much. I can't do it all." Although she clarified her ability to handle the tasks – "I mean, I can do it all" – the limitations of her own time remain a burden – "but I can't do it all." When considering new initiatives, a South Dakota owner emphasized the importance of work-life balance. "It's two full-time (employees), me and my partner, and then we have a part-time reporter, a part-time proofreader and a part-time archivist. And these are all of the people. … I'm strained," he said. "It's like, well, I would like to go to bed at some point or have dinner with the family or go do something fun for myself. That'd be great. I'd like to leave the paper behind please for an evening." He added later, "How much midnight oil do I want to burn?" The difficulties encountered by newsroom leaders extend beyond staffing limitations, encompassing time constraints that impact their professional commitments but also their personal lives.

Despite these issues faced by publishers, a number of them have contemplated, and, in some cases, executed strategies to generate new revenue. For instance, one Kansas publisher successfully implemented a community-driven cookbook and an associated cooking competition and has hopes to introduce a new festival or parade in her community. "We've thought about holding some kind of event at Christmas time, maybe get some sponsors on board," she said. Another Kansas publisher aspires to expand the organization's editorial offerings to reach a broader audience within her community. "I really want to pursue a podcast in Spanish," she said. "Some of our community is not literate in English or Spanish." She added that publishers need to "take a look at what your community needs – and do that." A Nebraska publisher recognized a need – and revenue potential – in offering website development and digital marketing services for her community. While the "websites are great revenue," she advised newsroom leaders to approach these endeavors with caution. "They are time-consuming because somebody always needs an update, and they always need an update when I don't necessarily have time to do it – on a Tuesday (production day for the newspaper)," she said.

> Website development, marketing, managing campaigns, they all have been good revenue. So, I think there's a lot of different avenues. … It's just a matter of watching that ROI – just to make sure that we're putting our efforts in the right avenues.

What was more prevalent were the reservations that newsroom leaders harbor when it comes to allocating their limited resources toward potential growth. These concerns became apparent during focus group discussions about hosting events. A South Dakota publisher feared the workload for her team. "I think an event seems very daunting for my size of staff," she said. "I can't imagine trying to put on something of significant size that would really bring in money." A North Dakota owner said she is active in the community Chamber of Commerce and assists in organizing events, like the annual July 4 fireworks show. "None of those things make any money," she said. "It's all volunteer-run, so I can't imagine if I was trying to pay staff to put together one of those things." Moreover, she emphasized the potential impact on their primary focus. "At the heart of it, I think it takes away from us producing what we are – we're in the news business," she said.

> We need to be spending our time producing news and advertising, with our current (business) model. When I think about an event, that's a completely different type of thing than we're trying to do. How many hours are we going to take away from the reporter and the layout person to try to do something? And at the end of the day, what are we going to end up with?

In general, publishers express concern about the uncertainty of possible financial returns that initiatives may yield and the diversion of resources from core offerings.

The tension between limited resources and potential growth has long been a challenge. This challenge is not lost on a veteran Kansas newsroom publisher who has witnessed it throughout her career. "I've seen over the 40 years that I've been pushed into (new initiatives in) journalism, sort of kicking and screaming – send out texts, send out faxes to everybody, send out announcements to their phones and things," she said.

> I don't know. It's just a lot of work. And how much money is it going to bring in, compared to your base product? If you have to take a person away from advertising or from news, and you only have two people – I mean, one in advertising and one in news – what's going to happen to your base product? That's my problem.

It is precisely this question, this problem, that ingrains reluctance among leaders to experiment, if they ever do.

Potential versus Perception

Newsroom leaders' deep-seated apprehension about audience perception of potential new revenue avenues creates an enduring tension that hampers progress and perpetuates a state of status quo. As previously discussed, leaders were wary of the audience's potential confusion or resistance if they transitioned away from a traditional subscription model. Further, they were anxious about a negative perception that could arise if employees were to devote time to engage in other pursuits, ultimately compromising the caliber of journalism. These fears of a negative perception stifle action, impede progress, and hinder meaningful change. Amidst the array of revenue-generating possibilities, none elicit as much apprehension regarding audience perception as the prospect of accepting donations for the news organization. With rare exceptions, newsroom leaders in our focus groups expressed opposition. The majority vehemently dismissed the idea, driven by concerns of compromised independence or tarnished reputation. While a few leaders exhibited some receptiveness, they firmly emphasized any potential support would hinge upon crucial factors, such as the identity of the donor and the magnitude of the donation. Notably, newsroom leaders also stated that other nonprofit organizations within their communities were in greater need of donations, diminishing the significance of their own news organization in the community landscape.

From the news leaders' perspectives, soliciting and accepting donations signifies a stark admission of ineffectiveness or failure within their current business practices, an unsettling revelation as they strive to project a façade of stability and staunchly avoid any hint of vulnerability in both their individual newspapers and the broader newspaper industry. One North Dakota leader emphasized that her primary objection in relation to donations is "pride," acknowledging the difficulty in recognizing the shortcomings of the existing business model. "It's hard to just swallow that and admit that, hey, the (business) model we're doing right now isn't working very well," she said.

> I am very sensitive to our reputation as an industry. … It's scary when we see all of the bad news, and I'm trying to not make it look like we're just a bucket with a hole in it that people are putting money in.

The news leaders forcefully emphasized their identity as businesspeople, leaving no room for doubt about their disinterest in donations. "I feel like we're kind of the wrong people to ask because we're business owners that get asked to donate everything," a female Nebraska owner said. "I think we're kind of like, 'What? No.' We wouldn't ever ask anyone to donate to us." Said another Nebraska leader of donations: "I'm totally uncomfortable with that," rejecting even the slightest notion of the idea. "I'm a businessperson," she said.

> I'm not very responsive to my insurance man coming down the street and asking me if I want to donate to his business. … I just feel like we have to figure out ways to pay for ourselves that justifies our existence. I think that's part of our responsibility as businesspeople and business owners.

Summing up the collective perspective, she later added, "The donation word isn't OK with what we do."

Modest contributions from readers, tacitly acknowledged as donations by the news leaders, proved more acceptable as these small sums emerged in conversations about readers voluntarily overpaying for their cost of their annual print subscriptions. A South Dakota publisher once had a customer ask about paying for four years' worth of a subscription. "I said, 'That's totally up to you. If you want to be on the list for four years, we'll take your money,'" she said. "I think they just wanted to give us more money, and that's OK with me. But I'm not comfortable, I guess, seeing it as a donation. I feel like it's a fair trade." Another South Dakota publisher said that he would "certainly accept" small, private donations to his news organization. "I have had a few customers, people who know us personally and people who we've interacted with, they've written us larger checks," he said of overpayments. "They've said, 'Hey, I really value your paper. … I really like what you guys are doing. So here, boom.'" However, he clarified his reluctance in initiating donation drives. "I don't see myself ever going to start a campaign," he said. "I mean, I am a for-profit business. So, on the whole, no." It was the same for a North Dakota publisher:

> I would maybe be more open to, when we send out renewal notices, having a line there where it's, "Here's what you need to pay for your subscription. If you want to donate an extra amount, here," and having it just as a part of what they're paying annually – versus a specific push, saying, "Hey, we need your money," she said.

"I think it's hard to imagine us doing a direct push for donations." Additionally, the perspective of the news leaders was significantly influenced by the value of the donation. A North Dakota publisher, for example, feared potential accusation of personal benefit and doubts regarding the proper utilization of donation funds. "If somebody wants to come into your counter and buy a newspaper for a buck and leave you a $5 and say, 'Keep the change,' that's cool," he said. However, he emphasized he would not solicit, nor accept, larger donations.

> (Say) I went on vacation or I bought a car. What is the public's perception, that, "Oh, my goodness, they're asking for money. It's not in the paper – it's lining the (owner's) pocket. He went on a vacation at my expense."

While some newsroom leaders exhibited a passive acceptance of small, private donations, they staunchly maintained their opposition to actively soliciting contributions, showcasing a complex, nuanced, and delicate dilemma.

While the amount of the donation is a significant factor, the source of the donations holds greater significance to news leaders, who overwhelmingly express fears of a perception of donor influence, particularly if accepting donations from politicians. A North Dakota publisher exemplified many others' concerns. "I think with the political climate we're in, that's really difficult to try and navigate that and help the average person understand," she said of a politician's donation.

> It's, "Oh, yeah, mm-hmm, typical media getting bought off by the politicians." … I really feel that it's important that we maintain that third party, that fourth estate sort of position. Anything that can be construed as the media being bought off by politicians, I really want to try and stay away from. That's the biggest thing.

She drew a distinction between a political donation and a political advertisement.

> People understand that politicians are going to buy advertising. I mean, how else do they get in front of the public? But when it comes to a direct donation to a for-profit business that's supposed to be unbiased and third party, I think that's where it gets tricky.

Ultimately, the North Dakota publisher said, for instance, if a state senator asked to donate to her publication, "I'd probably tell him, 'No, thank you.'"

The news leaders' concerns extend beyond politicians and include other stakeholders and business leaders within their communities. They perceive a clear distinction, both in their views and in the eyes of their audiences, between a business leader placing an advertisement and making a philanthropic donation. A South Dakota publisher had concerns about donors believing they "own" him. "When donations hit a certain amount, how much is it that they have influence with you?" he asked.

> That's the question. I want to remain objective here in my community. If certain members of my community, who I know are the wealthy landowners and business owners, if they came it to me with a very large check and said, "Here you go," would I take that money? Because sometimes I have to report about them. And sometimes not everything I report is positive. And so, do they own me? That's the thing.

In the same focus group, a veteran South Dakota publisher followed that comment and agreed, saying she would be uninterested in donations. "I can't see any way I would be in favor of doing anything about donations for the very reason that (he) was just speaking about, influence," she said. "Advertising is one thing. People need the paper to get their message out. They need the paper to have information available to the community. As a donation, to me, seems like something I would not want to get involved in." Recognizing the common occurrence of advertisers attempting to influence editorial content, a male Kansas news leader said of a hypothetical car dealership owner, "Is he going to twist my arm? Is he going to twist your sales rep? Yeah. He's going to bend our ear. But I think that they're not the same thing (as donations)." In stark contrast to her colleagues who staunchly opposed the notion of accepting donations, one Kansas publisher shared her success with soliciting donations. She secured two $10,000 contributions from a single business leader. "I was shocked," she said. "It very much helped us. He has been very outspoken to me about, 'You need to promote (donations) more.'" During the focus groups, she realized she stood in the minority, surrounded by counterparts who held reservations about donations. However, she passionately emphasized the potential of donations and urged others to consider the possibilities. "I do believe people will donate, if they believe in what you are doing," she said. "I think it is a direction we have to continue to work on." Focus group participants interrogated the Kansas publisher, asking direct questions about problems that they perceived would arise, notably the donor seeking influence on the editorial product. "Did you feel any pressure?" one asked. "None at all from this particular donor," she said. Such rare publisher decisions undoubtedly provoke scrutiny from news leaders across the country, viewed as nothing short of audacious at best and, at worst, unthinkable.

As briefly mentioned earlier, news leaders also express reluctance in accepting donations because they believe other organizations within their communities are in greater need. "I think the biggest issue for me is taking donation money that I think there are plenty of nonprofits doing great work in our community that could use it first," a female North Dakota publisher said. "I would rather that money go to them." A male North Dakota counterpart pointed out that all businesses, including the news organization, are struggling financially:

> If you're in a small town, everyone is standing there right now, going, "I could use a donation." I don't care if it's a hardware store. I don't care if it's a clothing store. They all need help. So that would be a road I would never walk down.

Another North Dakota leader agreed. "There are both nonprofits and for-profit businesses in our communities that have the same needs," she said, "and it becomes hard to justify why we need it over them." With such a perception, a conviction that other organizations are more worthy of donations, the leaders undermine the significance of their own news organization's value within the community.

In sum, despite the prevailing financial constraints that grip news organizations, news leaders resolutely maintain a disinterest in seeking donations as a means to move forward. "If you're needing donations," a Nebraska publisher said, "then up your advertising or subscription rates." Clearly against donations, she continued, "or find some other way to make money." A North

Dakota publisher agreed and shared a collective thought for how readers can support news organizations if they were considering donations. She said:

> If you don't have a subscription, buy a subscription. If you know someone that could use a subscription, give it to them as a gift. Put a birthday greeting in the paper for your friend, for your sister, for your mother. (Put) an announcement in the paper if you have a baby. It's paying for space in those regards. Or buy advertisements in the paper.

"This is the business model we're in now. I would rather have you use the mechanisms that are in place." In other words, the news leaders would rather perpetuate time-honored practices that have sustained news organizations for generations rather than consider a new avenue for revenue.

Summary

Through analysis of a survey of 100+ rural, weekly newspaper leaders and focus groups with 19 newsroom leaders in four U.S. states, this chapter presents an overall absence of innovation from news organizations concerning their financial practices. Despite dire headlines, distressing dilemmas, and the daunting lived experiences within their communities and newsrooms, news leaders are trapped in a state of inertia and paralyzed by their current circumstances. Their fears about potential short-term losses in readership and dwindling revenues hinder their ability to take steps toward long-term solutions. This aversion to risk and uncertainty has resulted in a reliance on an antiquated business model that has persisted for well over a century, leaving them seemingly adrift, waiting for clear guidance before navigating a path forward. For the cautious, yet willing, newsroom leaders, there exist compelling examples to emulate in their pursuit of business diversification, transformative strategies, and new revenue avenues. Indeed, that is the goal of this book and its experiment with Joey and Lindsey Young, as described in Chapter 5. What distinguishes bold leaders is their determination to take decisive action in safeguarding their future before it is too late. We argue leaders must recognize that believing nothing is wrong and remaining stagnant is not a viable choice for the future of local news.

Acknowledgment

This chapter is derived in part from the article "Revenue & Readership: Rescuing & Reviving Rural Journalism," published in *Journalism Practice* in March 2023, Copyright Taylor & Francis, available at https://www.tandfonline.com/doi/full/10.1080/17512786.2023.2183236.

4 Readers

Seeking Change

Teri Finneman

Creating a new business model for the newspaper industry requires more than just asking what publishers are willing to consider. The most critical component is whether consumers will support it. Therefore, after collecting responses from newspaper publishers to learn their views, the next step was to hear from readers to find out what today's consumers think in relation to paying for news. To keep answers comparable, the same four states were revisited: North Dakota, South Dakota, Nebraska, and Kansas. A sample of rural residents in each state responded to questions similar to those posed to the publishers in order to gauge their opinions on a business model for newspapers. Notably, they responded strikingly differently from the publishers, indicating a disconnect between weekly newspapers' financial strategies and what readers are willing to support.

Finding Rural Readers

To find a wide range of opinions, professional audience research company Coda Ventures conducted a survey to understand the perspectives of rural residents in the four states mentioned above. The company used a U.S. Census-based representation of participants to complete the survey in early 2022. To keep the survey focused on rural audiences, Coda Ventures reached participants in towns with populations under 10,000, thereby avoiding metro areas such as Fargo, Sioux Falls, Omaha, and Wichita. To recruit participants, Coda worked with another company, Schlesinger, which has a panel of millions of people who are prequalified and have agreed to take online studies. For this research, panelists received an email invitation to take the survey. Coda Ventures set quotas based on zip codes, age, and gender demographics. Respondents started the study by entering their zip code, gender, and age. If they met the quota qualification, they then continued with the survey. While certainly other demographic information may be useful, such as income, Coda Ventures noted age and gender were the best and most statistically sound quotas to use due to the challenges of acquiring the needed sample size and the widespread hesitancy of some survey participants to report personal financial information.

DOI: 10.4324/9781003414582-4

Beyond basic demographics, the survey asked a series of 13 questions related to participants' newspaper reading habits, their willingness to financially support the newspaper industry (and how), and their opinions on newspaper content. Questions were a mix of multiple choice, Likert-scale, and open-ended short answer. Queries included whether the participant would financially support their local newspaper beyond a subscription, if they would provide financial support if they knew their local newspaper was struggling to stay open, and what would make them more likely to financially support the newspaper. The survey generated 414 results: 103 from North Dakota, 100 from South Dakota, 108 from Nebraska, and 103 from Kansas. Most participants (327) live in communities with populations under 4,000, while 70 lived in communities over 4,000. Seventeen participants said they did not know their community's population. About 51% of respondents were female, a ratio in line with U.S. Census data of the time (50.5%). Broken down by age, 23.4% were 18–34, 28.7% were 35–54, 18% were 55–64, and 29% were 65 or older, resulting in an overrepresentation of senior citizens (Census and state demographics were about 17%). The researchers then ran cross-comparisons to further understand willingness to pay for local news within these rural populations.

Readers and Revenue Streams

The main question that the survey sought to discover was how likely rural residents would be to spend money on various revenue-generating strategies that could help support their local newspaper. Likert-scale questions asked participants about their level of willingness to provide financial support via each of these 12 strategies: taxpayer support, print subscriptions, ads, digital subscriptions, donations, events, memberships, e-newsletters, marketing services, graphic design services, office supplies, and/or commercial printing. Table 4.1 illustrates the breakdown of those who said they were "very likely" or "somewhat likely" to support these categories.

Events were the top choice by rural residents for providing additional revenue to newspapers, illustrating a strategy already made popular by news outlets such as *The Texas Tribune* and historically used by U.S. newspaper titans Joseph Pulitzer and William Randolph Hearst (see Moore & Gabriele, 2022). The popularity of this option is not surprising coming from rural areas where "there's nothing to do," and arguably provides an opportunity for newspapers to fill a central community engagement role in person, not just in print. The second option that rural residents were very likely or somewhat likely to support was print subscriptions. This adds further evidence that print is still a mainstay in rural America, not only out of habit but in part due to internet access issues that continue to impact remote communities. E-newsletters, memberships, and donations rounded out the top five – a striking contrast to the publishers, who ranked e-newsletters and memberships toward the bottom

Table 4.1 The percentage of rural residents who indicated they were "very likely" or "somewhat likely" to financially support newspapers through these various revenue-generating options. Across four central U.S. states, 414 people of varying demographics completed the survey.

Revenue stream	*Readers very likely/likely to support*
Events	54%
Print subscriptions	52%
E-newsletters	48%
Membership	41%
Donations	40%
Taxpayer support	40%
Office supplies	37%
Advertising (buy)	37%
Digital subscriptions	35%
Commercial printing	26%
Marketing services	23%
Graphic design services	21%

of their choices. Also of note is that digital subscriptions ranked substantially lower with readers (35%) than publishers (75%). While it might seem incongruous that readers desire innovative measures such as e-newsletters but do not seem to want digital subscriptions, this actually makes sense. Many rural news organizations utilize digital subscriptions that are essentially only a PDF version of the print product. Readers, historically, find PDFs of newspapers not engaging, not something worth much time (Ferrucci & Alaimo, 2020), and, therefore, not innovative.

A skeptical publisher may ask why they would want to pursue a strategy that "only" 40% or 54% support. In turn, we would argue that four out of ten or five out of ten people in the community appear willing to provide additional money the newspaper is not generating now, and 40% paying more is better than the current 0%. Furthermore, additional analysis of the most popular strategies found a number of rural residents chose the "undecided" box when considering their options. In other words, there is *potential* for newspapers to gain more revenue from these consumers if a convincing argument is made. With this in mind, Table 4.2 breaks down the top five strategies that rural residents preferred. This chart illustrates that about two-thirds of respondents would support or would consider financially supporting newspapers through events, memberships, e-newsletters, donations, or taxpayer support if given the opportunity to do so.

After they ranked the possible financial support options, rural residents were able to leave comments to help further understand why they made these choices and what would make them more likely to support their paper. Perhaps thinking their choice was self-explanatory, there weren't many comments

Table 4.2 This chart illustrates survey respondents who were very likely to support, somewhat likely to support, or undecided on a particular revenue stream.

Revenue stream	*Readers support or would consider*
Events	72%
Memberships	66%
E-newsletters	66%
Donations	64%
Taxpayer support	64%

about why events were so popular. However, a 55–64 Kansas woman said she "would support local events that sponsor the local paper." A male Kansas senior citizen said he would attend "some kind of special event they would sponsor." Two North Dakota women in the 18–34 age group from different towns also said they would go to fundraiser events to help financially support their local newspapers. An 18–34 Nebraska man in a town of 3,001–4,000 wanted to see the newspaper be more interactive with the community, a comment echoed by a 35–54 Nebraska man in a town under 500 who wanted the newspaper to ask readers more often what they care about. This suggests even a small event like coffee shop hours with the editor could be helpful in remote communities. The events revenue strategy goes beyond the tightly controlled boundaries of practice that most contemporary newspapers are accustomed to, yet these readers are pushing for innovation to entice them to provide more financial support for local news. Events would also help newspapers return to their historical role serving as a central hub for the community.

No one left comments relating to memberships despite it being the second most popular option. Memberships were described on the survey as "a perk beyond a subscription." It is possible in this era of Netflix, Amazon, and gym memberships that readers have some concept of what a membership program involves, although this is an area that would benefit further from audience focus groups. Readers were clearer, however, in explaining why they chose the e-newsletter option. A Kansas woman between the ages of 55 and 64 in a town of 2,001–3,000 people said she wanted to get news more than once a week, indicating it was no longer sufficient to wait for the weekly printed paper to know what was going on. A Nebraska man in the 18–34 age group had the same suggestion: "My local newspaper doesn't print often enough to really keep up with current events unless they are super specific to the region. Maybe if they put out a paper more often." An 18–34 Nebraska woman also wanted "more than a once-a-week newspaper." Two South Dakota readers also made comments to "be more timely on the info" and "have it come out daily instead of weekly." A North Dakota senior citizen wanted her news to "be more up to date," while another North Dakota woman wanted the paper "showing up before news is old." This is a positive for weeklies that readers have an urgency for local news and should prompt consideration of an e-newsletter that delivers news more often. After many weeklies had to operate like dailies during COVID-19 (Finneman & Thomas, 2021), it is not surprising that readers grew accustomed to receiving local news more often. This suggests that readers are more apt to want innovation and a local news service that adapts to the 21st century with more timely content.

Reader Motivation for Financial Support

As we discuss in greater detail in the next two sections, the majority of people who took the survey were willing or willing to consider providing more financial help to their newspaper. Before we discuss *who* said this, we discuss *why* rural residents felt this way. Two main themes emerged on how to better financially engage readers: appealing to their altruism and improving newspaper content. We then briefly discuss the minority who did not want to help and why.

Altruistic Motivation

Many respondents said they would financially support their newspaper simply because they wanted to be of help, a trend that emerged across states, age ranges, and town size. A Kansas man between the ages of 18 and 34 wrote, "If they were in financial trouble, I'm always here to help the community." A 35–54 Nebraska woman said, "just knowing they need it would make me want to support them." An 18–34 South Dakota woman said she would help because "I like to support local business." A 35–54 Nebraska man would pay more "to make sure it stays open for business so others can keep their jobs." A North Dakota male senior citizen said, "I would do whatever I could financially to help out our local paper." An 18–34 Nebraska man said, "The fact that I support local business, they're important." A 35–54 Kansas woman said she would pay more "if I knew they were struggling financially."

Some shared personal stories of altruistic attachment, such as a 55–64 Kansas man from a town of 3,001-4,000: "They have been a fixture in the community since my grandmother was young. Myself, as well as many of my friends, are already prepared to do practically anything to support our paper. My town is like that." A 35–54 North Dakota man in a town of fewer than 500 people said he would help "just to keep it going in a small town … I love all our small-town news, so I'd do all I can to keep it going." An 18–34 South Dakota woman in a town of 1,001–2,000 said she would help "because we all enjoy having a paper and I don't think I'd like it if they didn't exist cause I wouldn't know anything for my kids for school." A senior citizen South Dakota woman from a town of 4,001–5,000 said "knowing they needed help, I would gladly support our local newspaper and would also do some fundraising to help out." These responses indicate that readers are indeed willing to go beyond the boundaries of the newspaper industry's current business model if given an opportunity to do so and are made aware of the need for their increased financial support. This contrasts drastically with publishers who were not willing to consider donations or who were not open to providing new avenues for readers to pay more.

Consumer Motivation

Many survey respondents indicated they would give more financial support if newspapers made changes to improve service. This illustrates that newspapers need to do more than just change fundamental revenue streams but also consider changes to longtime journalistic content routines to bring in more money. Readers indicated this through a variety of survey responses: (1) through comments in response to the question, "What would make you more likely to financially support your local newspaper?"; (2) by reviewing a list of a dozen newspaper beats and checking all that they favored when asked, "What topics are you most interested in your local newspaper covering?" (Table 4.3); and (3) through comments in response to the question, "How could your local newspaper improve its content?"

In regard to content priorities, rural readers' top choice was obituaries/birth announcements/marriage announcements, which have long been staples of weekly newspapers. Feature stories ranked second, while a "things to do" calendar and crime reports tied for third. A notable finding was that only 27% checked that they were interested in opinion content. In fact, based on the comments provided, some readers suggested that editors giving opinions in the paper made them less likely to support it, particularly if the editor was

Table 4.3 These are the beats that rural readers said they care about the most.

Type of content	*Reader favorability*
1. Obits/births/marriages	57%
2. Features	54%
3. Things to do (tied)	53%
3. Crime (tied)	53%
4. Business	43%
5. Ads	40%
6. Weather	39%
7. Sports	38%
8. Local government	38%
9. Education	34%
10. Senior citizens	28%
11. Opinion	27%
12. Religion	18%

perceived as being liberal to conservative readers. A Kansas senior citizen in a town of fewer than 500 people wrote she wanted to see "a change of attitude of the newspaper. Lately they have been insensitive and rude in some of their editorial content." A female Nebraska senior citizen in a town of 2,001–3,000 wanted her newspaper to be more nonpartisan, "but that's probably asking too much in this area." A 35–54 North Dakota man in a town of 501–1,000 said he wanted a new editor: "I come from a very conservative area, but the local paper [name redacted] has a quite liberal Democrat for its editor." A 35–54 Nebraska man from a town of under 500 "would like to see more relevant information and less bias opinions." A North Dakota female senior citizen in a town of 501–1,000 put it directly: "less editor opinion." About half of these respondents knew the journalists at their newspaper, while the other half did not. Regardless, the low number of people who quantitatively expressed interest in opinion content is worthy of additional reflection by weekly editors who, for centuries now, have relied on opinion as a normative practice.

Many readers said they were fine with their newspaper's news content or were not sure what else could be done to improve it. However, it was also clear that a strong subset of readers wanted to see improvements before they would pay more for the paper. Some suggested adding more business reporting, local history articles, children's pages, coupons, comics, and crossword puzzles. An 18–34 Nebraska woman wanted to see more stories that appealed to her age range, a comment echoed by two other Kansan women and a Nebraska man of the same age bracket. An 18–34 Kansas man put it most succinctly when he said he wanted to see "funner things" in the paper. Similarly, a Nebraska woman in the same age range wanted to see her newspaper expand "its content from what it's been for 300 years." Even a Nebraska senior citizen was bored with her newspaper, advising to "cover more local stories, not the same content every issue."

Several comments from across states wanted to see *more* content in their weekly newspaper, illustrating a continued level of importance for local news. A 35–54 male Nebraska man from a town of 1,001–2,000 had a full wish list:

> For them to write more about town events, people's stories, the marriage license report, the courthouse report, the violations report, the births, marriages, not just opinions and sports – write the stories of the people! And not just the well-known maybe dig a little and show light in the dark for some!

A female senior citizen in Kansas wanted better coverage of local events, like city council meetings. A North Dakota female senior citizen from a town of 1,001–2,000 said, "I would support and subscribe to the newspaper if it had any substantial content besides a couple of editorial columns and the school sports." A Nebraska female senior citizen said she would support the paper if it "actually ha[d] local news in it," a comment that came up from multiple people. Another North Dakota female senior citizen wanted to see "more local news in it." Others complained about insufficient coverage of schools and sports. "It needs to truly be a local paper, not a few articles mixed into articles from the town 60 miles away. There are very few local stories from this arrangement," a Nebraska female senior citizen in a town with fewer than 1,000 people wrote. "Right now, it seems like the only thing they cover is the police report," a 55–64 Nebraska man in a town of 3,001–4,000 wrote in his commentary about wanting more local news. A 55–64 North Dakota woman said her local paper "need to have more relevant content, not old news or items of interest only to a handful of people." A 55–64 Kansan man complained about the quality of the writing and photography in his newspaper in a town of over 5,000 people. Two Kansas woman said they wanted to see better written stories, while another wanted "a more diverse look at the town." It became clear in these comments that the same old content habits in weekly newspapers were growing stale, suggesting editors should do more to ask current readers how to enliven the paper. Furthermore, readers are not interested in non-local content and want their hometown paper to focus on more local news.

Finally, we briefly touch upon the 25% minority who were unwilling to do anything to provide additional financial help to their local paper. About two dozen people (6% of the sample) left comments indicating that they didn't have enough money to pay more for the newspaper. Some mentioned they are senior citizens on a limited income, thereby posing the potential for newspapers to consider offering a senior citizen subscription rate. However, this also indicates that newspapers need to do a better job – like any other business – explaining the cost and benefit of the product. Many weeklies charge $1 an issue, breaking down to 14 cents a day to support local news. Therefore, most arguments about affordability are dubious at best and, we argue, the industry must do better at addressing this myth. Additionally, 66 of the 414 respondents (16% of the sample) wrote there was "nothing" anyone could do to make them more likely to give money to their local newspaper. About a dozen additional negative responses referred to the words truth, liberal, biased, and/or Democrat, with men three times as likely to voice concerns related to liberal media than women did. In the current political climate, this is not surprising and, again, this was a minority. We explore next in more detail the majority of respondents who were willing to help or consider it.

Who Supports Local News?

Across all four states, readers were twice as likely to say they would provide additional funding if they knew a journalist. This was particularly striking in South Dakota where 62.5% of those who knew a local journalist would pay beyond a subscription compared to 26.5% who don't know one. Interestingly, only one in five people in towns with a population of 500 or fewer knew a journalist, providing further evidence of a disconnect between journalism and the most rural portions of the United States. About half of residents in towns of 1,000–4,000 knew their local journalists. Notably, a Nebraska woman in the 18–34 age group from a town of 1,001–2,000 noted that newspapers should do more outreach so that people in the community know who the journalists are. She suggested "*occasional meet and greets with the employees. Easier to partner with people rather than a business.*" This comment provides further insight into why the membership and events options were popular with respondents. Although historically there has been an industry-implemented barrier between editorial and advertising, these findings emphasize the role that journalists themselves play in serving as ambassadors for bringing in additional revenue, and the need to innovate from tightly controlled boundaries of practice.

We also broke down by age and gender those who would be willing to provide more financial help to their newspaper if they knew it was struggling and found men (47.3%) more supportive than women (34%). Why that is the case is unclear and worthy of future analysis. Another notable finding breaks the common belief that only older Americans support newspapers. Residents ages 18–54 across all four states were more willing to help their newspaper than those over age 55 (102 "yes" answers versus 66 "yes" answers). Specifically, the 18–34 demographic that most assume does not support newspapers provided 29% of the "yes" answers. The "dad" demographic of men ages 35–54 was most supportive of paying more to help local news. Overall, these findings contradict assumptions used as reasons to cling to historical normative practices and illustrate modern readers as a market force that supports innovation.

From a statewide perspective, 38% of all respondents in South Dakota, Nebraska, and Kansas said they would help if their newspaper was financially struggling, with 49% of North Dakotans agreeing (Table 4.4). An additional 25% of respondents in North Dakota and South Dakota, and 37% in Nebraska and Kansas, were unsure. In other words, between 62% and 75% of respondents in each state would either help or consider helping their newspaper if they knew it was financially struggling. This highlights the critical importance of newsrooms being transparent with readers about their finances and pursuing additional revenue strategies.

Table 4.4 Survey respondents were asked: If you knew your newspaper was struggling to stay open, would you be willing to provide more financial support? They were given the options: yes, unsure, or no.

State	*Would pay more*	*May pay more*	*Won't pay more*
North Dakota	51%	24%	25%
South Dakota	38%	24%	38%
Nebraska	38%	37%	25%
Kansas	38%	37%	25%

Summary

Resistance to innovation is costing newspapers additional revenue from readers not bound by historic restrictive practices and limiting potential to increase news coverage that would attract further readers and revenue. Overall, our study found readers are most supportive of events, print subscriptions, e-newsletters, memberships, and donations. The strong support for events correlates with a desire in many rural communities for more things to do. This potential revenue stream can easily be paired with a membership program that offers special access to events in addition to a newspaper subscription. Furthermore, readers who knew a journalist were twice as likely to say they would pay more to support their newspaper than those who did not. Therefore, events serve as an opportunity for journalists to meet more people in their community while also generating more revenue. The myth that young people do not care about news and that senior citizens are the backbone of the newspaper industry was also busted with this study as residents ages 18–54 across all four states were more willing to financially help their newspaper than those over age 55. This suggests more innovative funding opportunities and content updates would better serve the future of local news. Newspapers would also be well-advised to be more transparent with their readers about the state of the industry and the need for more reader support. Two-thirds of readers in this survey said they would either help or consider helping their newspaper if they knew it was financially struggling.

As a whole, the reader results stand in direct contrast not only to publishers' perceptions of what readers would support, but also publishers' willingness to enact mechanisms to diversify revenue streams. Limitations to the reader data include the narrow geographic area surveyed and its predominantly white sample, as Census data notes the populations in these four states are 84–88% white. Future research should further gauge attitudes from publishers and readers in more diverse areas. Overall, though, despite potential limitations, this reader survey shows a fundamental disconnect between the publishers of rural newspapers and those who read them, which potentially imperils the financial viability of these civic institutions.

Acknowledgment

This chapter is derived in part from the article "Revenue & Readership: Rescuing & Reviving Rural Journalism," published in *Journalism Practice* in March 2023, Copyright Taylor & Francis, available at https://www.tandfonline.com/doi/full/10.1080/17512786.2023.2183236.

References

Ferrucci, P., & Alaimo, K. I. (2020). Escaping the news desert: Nonprofit news and open-system journalism organizations. *Journalism*, *21*(4), 489–506.

Finneman, T., & Thomas, R. J. (2021). "You had to be reporting constantly": COVID-19's impact on US weekly newspapers' journalistic routines. *Newspaper Research Journal*, *42*(3), 330–345.

Moore, P., & Gabriele, S. (2022). *The Sunday paper: A media history*. University of Illinois Press.

5 Press Club

Implementing Change

Teri Finneman and Nick Mathews

Harvey County Now Editor Adam Strunk had a clear answer when asked in early 2022 what had prevented his newspaper from altering its business model and considering a membership strategy:

> Running a company and trying to keep a company staffed and trying to get papers out every week, and trying to deal with every bit of bullshit we deal with, like, yeah. It would be great to, like, if we had a pile of free time, heck yeah, let's do all this shit.
>
> But it's like, I've gotta get a paper out every week. How are we gonna get someone at this local county commission meeting? It's not like, "Ooh. I'm gonna spend a day of my week setting up this fun little club." It's, yeah. So, it's a day-to-day grind.

His answer aligned with the feedback provided in the focus groups in Chapter 3 and with anecdotal stories of why newspapers have struggled to change their business models. It is why the next stage of this study – the experiment – was so critical to implement and record how *Harvey County Now*, a live working weekly newsroom, would adapt when required to change its model for an entire year.

In November 2021, the researchers approached Joey Young to ask if his newspaper company, Kansas Publishing Ventures, would be the test site for a business model theory. The project was part of an innovation grant funded by the journalism school at the University of Kansas. Joey had a reputation as a young, energetic publisher not afraid to speak his mind and confront the industry's challenges. He started *Harvey County Now* from scratch and developed a scrappy, loyal team with a commitment to local news. During an oral history at the start of the COVID-19 pandemic, he stuck out as a newspaper owner planning to furlough himself rather than his employees if cuts had to be made.

Neither he nor the researchers knew what business model his staff would be asked to operate when they agreed to partner to try to create an international model that other newspapers could use. His team was just coming off

DOI: 10.4324/9781003414582-5

a big decision that had generated much discussion in the newsroom. They decided to raise the subscription price of *Harvey County Now* from $50 to $60 a year – or from 96 cents to $1.15 an issue – starting in January 2022. Despite concerns they would lose subscribers, however, circulation remained steady.

This chapter details how *Harvey County Now* adjusted its business model to incorporate what became known as Press Club. This section also explores lessons learned when trying to incorporate change at the *Hillsboro Free Press*, another one of the company's newspapers. To be clear, Kansas Publishing Ventures maintained its current revenue model throughout the experiment. By the end, however, the new revenue strategies that formed the theory were engrained in the staff's day-to-day routines and brought in an additional $10,000, or 2% of the newspaper's overall income from July 1, 2022, to July 1, 2023, in the pilot year. Although the number looks small, the next two chapters explain the significance of it for the paper's future.

Over the course of 15 months, the researchers conducted oral histories and observations in person and over Zoom with the team as it worked in real time to adapt a theory to the practical newsroom. Using those oral history transcripts from April 2022 to June 2023, this chapter illustrates the trial-and-error progression of how the staff both practically and psychologically evolved as they implemented change. Furthermore, we explore how the team perceived the model's effects on the organization's credibility and relationship with the community. We begin by introducing the main characters in this experiment, referring to them by first name due to their own informal nature.

Who Is *Harvey County Now*?

Joey will tell you right away that he is not a normal newspaper owner. He was 27 when he bought his first Kansas weekly newspaper, *The Clarion*, in a town of fewer than 1,000 people. He was 37 and owned four weeklies when he agreed to participate in this experiment. Since starting Kansas Publishing Ventures, Joey said he has had a "throw stuff at the wall and see what sticks mentality" with no fear of trying new things. "If we want to move forward in this industry, we can't just keep patting ourselves on the back about how great we are," he said. "We gotta get in the muck. We gotta be a part of the community."

He also differed from other newspapers in that he wasn't nearly as dependent on advertising to keep the company operating. In early 2022, about 35% of Kansas Publishing Ventures' revenue came from display advertising, 23% from circulation, 5% from preprint inserts, 7% from legals, and 30% from custom printing and technology services. He has been willing to add different revenue streams because he believes strictly relying on display and classified advertising, circulation, and legals is not a sustainable model. Although his current model isn't as dependent on advertising as other weeklies, we argue this doesn't dilute the applicability of this experiment to other newspapers.

The overall goal is to illustrate whether specific strategies can boost the bottom line for a weekly newspaper. By trying this business model experiment, Joey hoped to increase the pay of his staff to help with retention and to consider additional hiring.

In early 2022, Kansas Publishing Ventures had 19 full- and part-time employees, not including freelancers, across its four newspapers. The ownership group includes Joey's wife, Lindsey Young, as well as Adam Strunk and Bruce Behymer. Lindsey, who was 39 when the experiment began, grew up in a Kansas town of 1,100 people. She majored in communication and was a student media editor in college but then became a high school teacher for ten years. After she met Joey, she began helping him in the newsroom and eventually joined the company full time. She describes herself as the "Mom" of the group and is detail-oriented. Adam, who was 31 when the experiment began, is editor of *Harvey County Now*. He grew up on a farm outside of Wichita and first met Joey when he worked as an intern at *The Clarion.* Initially planning to work his way up to a metro newspaper, Adam instead agreed to join Joey's team full time in 2013 and is now a minority owner in Kansas Publishing Ventures. Very devoted to the reputation of the newspaper, he considers the impact on the newsroom first and foremost. Bruce, who was 55 when the experiment began, is advertising director and also grew up with a family farm background. His first advertising job was for the *Newton Kansan*, which is now a competitor of *Harvey County Now.* He eventually ended up at the *Hillsboro Free Press* working for the owner prior to Joey taking over. When Joey bought the *Free Press*, he asked Bruce to be a minority owner. Referred to within the company as "marketing dude," he is known for his relationship-building in the town. Tommy Hornbeck worked for the company providing technology support but left Kansas Publishing Ventures midway through the experiment year to take a different job. The team as a whole is extremely tight knit, ending the work week with what they call "Beer Friday."

As for the newspapers themselves, *Harvey County Now* has a weekly circulation of about 4,000 and is based in Newton, Kansas, a community of about 20,000 people near Wichita. The newspaper usually runs between 24 and 30 pages and has a hard paywall for its web stories. Joey launched the newspaper in 2015 as a competitor to the then GateHouse-owned *Newton Kansan* to provide a locally owned alternative. At the start of this experiment, *Harvey County Now* had eight full-time employees and a handful of part-time employees and freelancers.

The *Hillsboro Free Press* is a free 8–12-page shopper (total market coverage) that goes to 5,500 households across its county. The paper is about 50% advertising and 50% newshole. Still, Lindsey said the *Free Press* is well read as evidenced by the calls that they get if the paper is late. Hillsboro has about 3,000 residents and is 25 miles from Newton. The community is home to a small private Mennonite college. The *Free Press* has two full-time and several part-time employees. It competes with a paid newspaper, the *Marion County Record.*

Kansas Publishing Ventures also owns *The Clarion* (circulation 1,100), which was not part of the experiment. The company owned the *McPherson News Ledger* (circulation 1,600) but sold it in early 2023.

Joey, who works 55–60 hours a week, said his company is profitable even with two of his newspapers in the (now rare) environment of competing against other papers within the same towns. "So, I don't wanna have to hear a bunch of people saying, 'We don't have time,' or 'We don't have enough revenue,'" he said of publisher excuses to not try a different business model. "You just have to step back and change some of what you're doing and think about what gaps in your community you can help fill, and what makes sense for the newspaper to fill."

Getting Started: Forming the Experiment

The leadership team of Kansas Publishing Ventures met with the researchers over Zoom in April 2022 to officially discuss what business model strategy they would try. Since agreeing in November 2021 to be the experiment site, Joey had been kept informed in the subsequent months how the business model theory was progressing so that the team wouldn't be taken by surprise concerning what to expect. The April meeting focused specifically on asking the staff members their thoughts on the event, e-newsletter, membership, and donation strategies that rated as top options in the reader data (detailed in Chapter 4). The staff was adamant, however, that they did not want to experiment with donations, provoking a reaction similar to that generated during the publisher focus groups (detailed in Chapter 3). Joey said he is open-minded in general but believed a for-profit newspaper should run as a business, not a charity. "If we're asking people for money, we wanna provide a service for that money," he said. "There's an exchange of goods or services. I don't feel great about people giving us money just for, I don't know." The community already has plenty of nonprofits doing fundraisers and asking for donations, he said. Lindsey also didn't want to use the donation strategy, saying it felt like "a dirty word" and that it would bother her to not provide something extra in exchange. Adam felt donations would create a perception problem of people trying to buy their way into the news. He also feared it would look like newspapers weren't providing enough value, so they had to ask for a handout, which he saw as sending a bad message to advertisers. He said they would put a disclaimer in the paper that it wasn't their idea to ask for donations if the researchers required them do it.

Realizing the project's success depended on the staff fully buying in over the next year, the researchers agreed to limit the experiment to events, e-newsletters, and memberships. From there, Joey said he quickly got excitement from the team. The staff already had some experience hosting a citywide event featuring bands and barbecue, but its prior e-newsletter attempts had not been successful. Therefore, he said they looked forward to delving more into these strategies. One concern, however, was the researchers' directive that the experiment needed to be conducted in two of their newspaper communities: Newton and Hillsboro. Joey said all the company's owners live in Newton and, even though Hillsboro was only 25 miles away, the connections weren't as strong. This was further compounded by the differing editorial models of the two newspapers and the differing personalities of the communities. Still, he believed the business model would help fill gaps in both communities and enhance the newspaper company. Joey was "incredibly confident" at the beginning of the experiment that the new business model strategies would work. "But if you asked anybody in the company, they would say that's not really all that different from where I normally am," he said, laughing.

> We don't expect to fail with this. We plan on going in with a really solid plan, adjusting that plan as it needs to be, and promoting the hell out of it. So, I really do think that this can be a successful model for our company.

Over the next few months, the staff committed to having lunch together every Friday to brainstorm how to incorporate e-newsletters, memberships, and events. Although there were informal check-ins with the researchers at times, Kansas Publishing Ventures was responsible for figuring out the details of how to make the model work. Lindsey kept detailed meeting minutes of what they discussed and what the assigned action items were for each team member. The staff began reaching out to key local stakeholders and advertisers to discuss the pending changes.

In this chapter, we outline how the business model progressed over the course of a year at *Harvey County Now* and the *Hillsboro Free Press.* Their story was captured through a series of 18 oral history interviews conducted by the researchers and through the team's meeting minutes. All materials are housed at the Kansas Historical Society. Ultimately, *Harvey County Now* streamlined the three initiatives to work as one model within the Press Club brand. However, we break them down as individual items here not only for readability but for those who may want to try just one initiative first (Figure 5.1).

The Model: Press Club

When deciding how to approach a membership model, the staff identified what they saw as a gap in Newton – the lack of opportunities for young people to socialize outside of a bar. Therefore, they began thinking how they could create an exclusive social group for newspaper subscribers that had corporate sponsors. "It would be an interesting new revenue stream for the paper but, even more important than that, I think the beauty of the membership model is that you create a fervent fan club," Joey said. Adam said he

August 4, 2022 Harvey County Now **OPINION**

It's not always easy to make friends as an adult

I am not from Newton. I didn't grow up in Harvey County, and outside of Harvey County Now, I haven't one connection to the whole community. Without this newspaper, I probably wouldn't know a soul in Newton or in Harvey County outside of my stint as a reporter for the Harvey County Independent when I was in my early 20s.

My wife and I grew up in Reno County, both in small towns, and most of our family and childhood friend networks still reside out there.

Moving to Newton was oddly scary. I had a network in Hutchinson. I had lots of friends and family to lean on if I wanted to go out to dinner, play fantasy football, have folks over for game night or whatever. It wasn't hard to be social in Hutchinson for me.

That wasn't the case in Newton. In a lot of ways it still isn't, even years after we have called Harvey County our home.

It's sometimes awkward to try and turn business relationships into friendships, even if many of them border that already. It isn't always smooth to see if someone you know professionally wants to go grab beers or hang out and watch football.

That is probably why, if you are a longtime reader of this opinion section, you catch a lot of references to Adam, the editor of Harvey County Now, and I and our spouses all hanging out in our free time.

Adam and I were friends before we became teammates at the newspaper. It was easy to hang out as we had a lot in common, and when moving to Newton, I have leaned heavily on that friendship as a social outlet.

It's hard to make new friends when

you are an adult—especially when there is a serious lack of social gathering spaces that are open after 5:30 p.m. in this town.

So how is someone supposed to make friends and socialize here? It's a good question, and it's one that we felt needed a solution, not just for the town's viability to bring in younger professionals, but just for my personal sanity.

A lot of folks have asked what the mission of Press Club is. If you have read this far into my column, I think you are starting to get the idea.

The mission is simple: we want to connect folks and make it easier to be social in a community that has no shortage of non-profits but a huge shortage of outlets just for the purpose of socializing.

That is why Press Club isn't political. It's not a civic group, either. It's just a reason to make friends and socialize for the sake of socializing.

We have held two open-to-the-public mingles at the Harvey County Now office in Newton, and both were well attended. We ate some snacks, drank a few brews, and socialized. It was nice. I even met some new people.

Now that we have dipped our toes in the water, we want to do more, though. So if you have signed up for our Press Club e-mail list, you will start seeing more than just monthly mingles on the calendar. We are going to have a group dinner in mid-August and plan to organize more later. We are finalizing a field trip to El Dorado and Walnut River Brewing Company for October. We are going to try to organize some teams to compete at Newton Recreation events, and we are even going to see if we can get a bar trivia team or two out to Moxie's on a Thursday night in the near future.

The idea behind Press Club is just infrastructure to hang out with folks who are interested in getting to know their neighbors and also happen to support the newspaper. If you have questions about it, let me know. If you are interested but not ready to sign up just yet, that is OK, but sign up to get the weekly e-mails so you know what is going on, and maybe you will pull the trigger soon.

Just like when we launched Blues, Brews and Barbecue years ago, we took a leap of faith and prayed folks would come and not just leave us hanging out in Athletic Park by ourselves for the evening.

And just like seven years ago when we launched this newspaper, I am asking again to take a leap of faith and become a founding member of something new and exciting. I would really appreciate the support, as if I don't make some new friends soon, Adam is going to get sick of me.

-Joey Young is the publisher of Harvey County Now. He can be reached at: joey@kspublishingventures.com

Figure 5.1 In August 2022, Joey Young ran a column in *Harvey County Now* to introduce his readers to Press Club, a new community-focused model aimed at bringing in additional revenue to the newspaper and building relationships. Courtesy of Kansas Publishing Ventures.

saw value in the membership strategy as an opportunity to get face-to-face with people who might not have known the newspaper staff otherwise. "And again, the better you know a journalist, the more likely you are to keep subscribing and supporting a local paper," he said. He also saw potential in finding out story ideas by gathering people to chat. "The more you make *Harvey County Now* the place everyone goes for any kind of community engagement, like, that's freakin' awesome, like, that's what you want," he said. "That's what papers used to be and that's returning that weight from maybe social media, some of these Facebook groups, to the newspaper. So, I like that."

During Friday team lunch meetings in spring 2022, the staff brainstormed how the details of what they called Press Club would work, including how to recruit members, set pricing, and give value to sponsors. Adam mentioned a recent story about brain drain in town and thought talking about that with potential sponsors would show the newspaper was doing something to help. Joey also thought the club serving as a recruitment and retention tool was a good way to frame the idea to businesses. He said they determined early on they were going to "stay in our lane" and try not to step on other community organizations' toes with their plans. While the local Chamber hosts events for the business community during the day, there aren't activities at night. Press Club, on the other hand, aimed to attract a mix of local residents in the early evening for snacks, drinks, and conversation. Kansas Publishing Ventures decided to have a set date of the third Thursday of the month and schedule it so people could go straight from work to what became known as "the monthly mingle." Lindsey said newspapers already have business and community connections, "so Press Club is a way for us to be able to bring those two together even more than we already do with just, you know, strictly print advertising." Like Adam, she was optimistic that the club mingles would result in more story ideas, buy-in from the community, and subscription sales. "So, it is a time commitment [for the newspaper's staff], but I think it's something that's so worthwhile because it's such a good connection with the community," she said.

To publicize the effort, Joey wrote a column in the paper explaining what Press Club was, Bruce created house ads, Tommy added a new Press Club section on the website, Lindsey redesigned the subscriber renewal notices and included an FAQ about Press Club on the back, graphic designer Shelley worked on a logo, and Joey and Bruce began talking about Press Club while out on regular advertising calls (Figure 5.2). Adam wrote a front-page story about their work that featured the researchers and started a spreadsheet with the names of people to personally invite to join Press Club to get an initial group of stakeholders involved. Adam said early feedback from the community was positive, making him optimistic. He personally called 20 people to tell them about the club, ask if they would be interested, and get input on what the club should look like. Other staff members also made personal calls and interactions rather than use email. They scheduled a launch party with appetizers and drinks for June 2022 at the newspaper office that would be open to the public to encourage sign ups.

The team decided Press Club members would need to pay the $60 annual newspaper subscription and then an additional $60 to join the club. Households could have the one subscription but then each member would need to pay an individual club fee. Corporate sponsors would pay $1,500. By doing so, they would receive 25 newspaper subscriptions and club memberships for their employees and be eligible to host a mingle at their business. *Harvey County Now* quickly established three initial corporate sponsors: two banks as well as the city through its Main Street program. Joey said early conversations

Figure 5.2 Joey and Bruce created this corporate sponsorship guide to discuss with advertisers while out doing their regular advertising calls. The sheet outlined what sponsors would get for $1,500. Courtesy of Kansas Publishing Ventures.

with potential sponsors were positive, leading him to think he could have charged more. He began conversations with businesses by saying newspapers should be doing community engagement and using the significant outreach they have through the press to connect people. "The word we're using is 'infrastructure.' We're trying to create infrastructure for there to be social interactions," Joey said.

> There aren't a lot of gathering places in Newton or in Hillsboro that are open in the evening, and so our goal is to kinda replicate the energy of a coffee shop, but, like, just move it around. It's like a pop-up bar.

Joey didn't create initial revenue goals because he wanted to focus first on getting key people in the community to sign up and be happy with what Press Club offered. He believed revenue would follow from there. He said if even 200 people paid an additional $60 a year, that would generate a lot of new money for the paper without much extra effort. The initial months putting the membership strategy in place amounted to about 10–15 hours per week spread across the team, or just a few hours per week per person, Joey said. He said he didn't feel like anyone on the staff was overwhelmed by the work needed to

Figure 5.3 This is an example of a house ad that *Harvey County Now* ran to let its readers know it was launching a Press Club program for them to join. Courtesy of Kansas Publishing Ventures.

create Press Club. Adam believed it would take even less time after the initial structure and publicity were set (Figure 5.3).

From an accounting perspective, Joey said they classified Press Club as a subcategory of circulation revenue in QuickBooks so that they could track it separately. He said Tommy came up with how to handle customers adding a Press Club membership in the middle of their subscription. Since Press Club was, essentially, doubling the cost of a subscription, the time left on a subscription was then cut in half. So, someone with 20 weeks instead had 10 weeks left and then would be sent a renewal for the full amount of Press Club and the subscription in 10 weeks. The company's philosophy even before Press Club is that everyone works in circulation, Joey said. Anyone who answers the phone needs to be able to address subscription questions, deliver newspapers, etc. Therefore, he said everyone in the company had to be versed on how to answer Press Club questions as well. Lindsey said it was important to make Press Club simple enough so that anyone in the office could explain it and anyone who called could understand it. Adam said he really wanted to push the overarching message that Press Club membership helps support local journalism.

Press Club FAQs

This guide from *Harvey County Now* illustrates how they explained Press Club to their readers.

What Is Press Club?

Press Club is a social group, brought to you by your friendly, community newspaper, *Harvey County Now*. We are non-political, non-religious, and aren't community service focused. Instead, our mission is to bring the Newton community together through a variety of events and functions.

How Do I Join Press Club?

There are two steps. First, your household must subscribe to a one-year (or longer) subscription to *Harvey County Now*. Then, the first person in your household (21 and older, please) who would like to be a Press Club member will pay an annual $60 (plus tax) membership fee, and any other people in your household will pay an annual $30 (plus tax) membership fee.

We Have Multiple People in Our Household Who Would Like to Join Press Club. How Does That Work?

You should maintain a one-year (or longer) subscription for your entire household. Then, the first membership for people living at that address will be the full $60 (plus tax), and any subsequent people living at that address will be $30 (plus tax). For example, if you're a two-person household, your total annual buy-in for Press Club will be $60 (plus tax) for a one-year subscription, $60 (plus tax) for person one and $30 (plus tax) for person two. That's only $150 (plus tax) for a whole year. Easy peasy.

What Benefits Do I Get from Press Club?

First of all, you have access to all Press Club events. Those include monthly mingles at local businesses where you'll get a chance to meet other local people, enjoy some snacks and beverages, and maybe win some door prizes. Other events include quarterly field trips, organized dinners or other get togethers, plus access to discounted events or other perks. Second, you will get our Press Club newsletter, which will keep you up to date on everything going on in Newton and the rest of the county. Third, you'll be a part of supporting one of the largest locally owned newsrooms in the State of Kansas.

Where Does My Membership Money Go?

Some of your membership dollars will go toward supporting Press Club activities, and the rest all will go toward supporting local, community journalism in Harvey County. You help maintain the jobs of local journalists and aid us in creating local coverage of issues, events, and people.

What if I Already Have a Subscription to Harvey County Now?

First of all, let us say that you're clearly one smart cookie. If you are already a subscriber, we'll prorate your current subscription along with your Press Club membership so that you will get a renewal notice for both at the same time. It's easier for you and for us. Contact Tommy at tommy@harveycountynow.com for more information.

Can My Employer Pay for This on My Behalf?

Absolutely. Many employers view groups like Press Club as an important benefit and retention tool. Contact us for more information or have your employer reach out, and we'll be happy to set up billing for them.

This FAQ Is Awful, and I Still Have Questions. What Should I Do?

Contact us through our website at https://harveycountynow.com/pressclub. We'll do our best to answer any additional questions you might have.

Ahead of Press Club's launch party in June 2022, Adam acknowledged the team was "a little bit stressed." He reflected on why newspapers don't change and the fear that comes with putting the publication's reputation on the line. "And when you go out with something completely new that could completely fail, you're putting your paper's name on it. And so, you're putting a personal feeling of, like, 'I'm going to be in front of my whole community failing,'" he said. "And so, that's really, I think, why you have a lot of resistance to change is because you are kind of afraid of that hit that your publication will take."

Lindsey also expressed some concern ahead of the experiment launch but for a different reason. She hoped the team would be able to stay focused and keep moving the experiment forward throughout an entire year. "We jump in with both feet, but we also tend to be a little ADD [attention deficit disorder] as a group," she said.

> Like, everybody loves to jump to the next new thing. I'm hoping that, because we're trying so many cool things with this membership, that it'll continue to be the next new thing [and keep the team's attention]. But I think, for me, my push will be to continue to refocus everybody and keep 'em on the path.

Adam further explained the team's dynamic by saying the newsroom has a motto of "no pet hogs," meaning ideas that seem good but are more involved than the return on investment or what the staff can do. Joey frequently uses the phrase "Is the juice worth the squeeze?" when describing cost-benefit ratios.

Bruce favored the membership model since he said his job as advertising director is "relationship selling." He saw the mingles as an opportunity to interact with businesses and subscribers. However, similar to Lindsey, he expressed concern about staff burnout and whether they would still have the energy for the club six months into it. "I have the luxury of being older 'cause I can look through that lens and go, 'You guys, I thought the same thing when I was 30. I'm looking at it different now. One day you're gonna get old too," he said laughing.

The day of the official Press Club launch, Lindsey admitted to being nervous but also excited. She said:

> I'm so ready to see how this changes, you know, our landscape and the community and just allows for a better infrastructure for people to meet each other and to just kind of grow those connections that just don't exist right now.

The overall success of Press Club will be determined by whether people continue to show up, Lindsey said. She hoped for 50–70 people to attend.

On the night of the first Press Club mingle in June 2022, the newspaper's office buzzed with about 60 people attending to chat, eat snacks, and drink beer (Figure 5.4). Joey said his favorite moment of the night was meeting new residents who didn't subscribe to *Harvey County Now* yet but heard about Press Club on social media and wanted to come to meet people in town. "To me, that's, like, absolute proof of concept," he said. "We had some people

Figure 5.4 Lindsey and Joey visit with a guest during the launch of Press Club at the *Harvey County Now* office in June 2022. About 60 people turned out for the first event. Courtesy of William O'Dell Crow.

show up from the business community, very positive feedback from the business community. One person in the business community specifically pulled me aside and said, 'This is something that's lacking in Newton.'"

While the team was pleased with the start of Press Club in Newton, the implementation of a similar concept in Hillsboro had been delayed. Joey decided early on that trying to implement Press Club in both Newton and Hillsboro at the same time was too much. He wanted to get a club going in Newton first and learn lessons from that launch before starting another. Joey said they discussed launching a Press Club concept in Hillsboro in fall 2022 and had met with stakeholders there about what would work in the community. Bruce wasn't sure if the social group model would work in more conservative Hillsboro. Lindsey said launching there would be different since the paper is free, not tied to subscriptions, and readers aren't used to sending in a check. "I think we're gonna really have to carefully explain, like, here's what benefits you get and here's why this matters," she said. "But I do think that there are people that recognize that, even though we're free, we are doing a community service for them, and I think that they would be willing to support that as well."

After the Launch

Six weeks after Press Club's launch in Newton, the staff found themselves immersed in the growing pains of creating a long-term strategy, not just a one-time event. There were about 40 initial Press Club memberships, a number that should have been closer to 130 but corporate sponsors were slow to provide the names of their employees who should be given memberships.

Although the initial plan was to host mingles at a different business every month, the team decided to keep hosting the events at the newspaper office until numbers grew so that a business wouldn't be disappointed with turnout. Press Club mingle attendance declined to about two dozen following the launch, so the staff tried to figure out the best way to communicate with members on how to attend the next events. In September 2022, Joey said they were surprised to learn that people don't check their work email often, so they had to put more house ads in the paper and create a members Facebook group to remind people when to attend (Figure 5.5). He also realized he needed to better communicate to corporate sponsors that Press Club was for their regular employees, not just a corporate perk for top managers. "I think, because this is a new concept, some of them are just slow to pick it up," he said. In the early stages of the experiment, he said his best advice to other publishers was

Figure 5.5 *Harvey County Now* frequently ran house ads to show members the benefits of Press Club. Courtesy of Kansas Publishing Ventures.

to immediately ask people the best way to communicate with them going forward at the time of sign up.

Still, three months into the experiment, the newspaper had generated $5,000 in new revenue with corporate sponsors and direct memberships with about $600 in expenses for hosting mingles. "We're very happy," Joey said in September 2022. "We haven't been spending a lot of money, and we also have been making a little bit, and we anticipate numbers going up as popularity gains." The team started drawings for prizes for Press Club members, like state fair tickets they received in an advertising trade-out, to further show membership benefits. Joey and Bruce asked to speak at a Chamber breakfast so that they could discuss Press Club with a larger audience as they continued to incorporate Press Club discussions into their regular advertising calls.

Joey acknowledged it's easy to back-track into old habits, and he felt himself cheerleading the team more than usual three months into the experiment to stay on track with growing the club. "The initial excitement has worn off at this point for staff members, so like now it's just trying to make sure there's continued excitement for it, which is literally [similar to] every single initiative we've ever done at the newspaper," he said.

> This is gonna take a little bit of time, and we're going to have to take two steps back sometimes to make one step forward, but as long as we're constantly trying to progress this concept, it'll be successful and will work. So, I recognize that not everything has been perfect. I would have liked things to go a little bit better. Like, I personally think it's insane when I had people who were like, "Well, we don't really check our work email." I'm like, "You what? You don't check your work email? Like how do you do anything?"

Although the quantitative numbers were slower than hoped and the initial communication strategies took time to develop, Joey said Press Club had a clear impact already on relationships with the community:

> There are people who were early adopters who I did not know and I had never met. There is this older gentleman who has come to every single one of our mingles, and he has gone out of his way to tell all of us how he looks forward to them and that he loves the newspaper.
>
> The more this thing grows, the more loyal – like everyone who joins is essentially – we have to view them as, like, in theory, a lifelong customer 'cause we can forge those relationships. So I would say the relationships have been significantly better. Um, with that said, some of the people early were who you'd expect. They were people who we already knew who liked the newspaper, who were perfectly happy to fork over extra money. We just needed to ask them. That's also awesome.

As the year progressed, The Press Club monthly mingles started venturing beyond the confines of the *Harvey County Now* newsroom and into the business headquarters of corporate sponsors. Joey and Lindsey only see positives in other businesses hosting the mingles. "There are almost no cons to having it elsewhere," Joey said. Lindsey also agreed:

> I honestly think it's all benefits. People like going into businesses, specifically businesses they don't normally go into. People are just naturally curious. So, I think it really does benefit the person who hosts, but it also increases attendance because people are like, "Oh, well, I wonder what the building looks like?" … I don't see any cons, especially from the newspaper's side of things.

"In a small town, it's amazing how many buildings you've never actually walked into even if you've lived there forever," Lindsey said. Perhaps the most successful corporate-sponsored monthly mingle was at a local insurance agency's office. "They have a tiny building, and it was just shoulder-to-shoulder in there," Lindsey said. "It was awesome. Like, it was just so full, and we had a really good time." Both Lindsey and Joey view the corporate-sponsored mingles as a win for both the businesses and the news organization. A major benefit is that it cuts down on the expenses for *Harvey County Now.* "When we host at other places, the attendance normally goes up, and then, on top of that, I don't have to buy food or beer – they do all that," Joey said.

> So, there's no cons to hosting elsewhere. I would say the pro of at least hosting at your office a couple of times is it does get people in your door. We want to make sure that we host every so often. We're never going to give away all the mingles.

Beyond revenue, the mingles have proven to be an invaluable asset to *Harvey County Now* from a journalistic perspective as well (Figure 5.6). Adam emphasized the advantages of establishing face-to-face connections with both community leaders and members during Press Club mingles. "It's helped me out a lot," he said. "There's a bank president we have in town. I knew him. He was always kind of a friend of the paper, but I didn't know him really well." The bank president was impressed with Press Club. "He thought Newton kind of needed something like that," Adam said. That, in turn, paved the way for the news organization to forge a strong relationship with one of the key stakeholders in the community. "That stronger relationship might extend to advertising. That stronger relationship might extend to (journalism)," Adam explained. For instance, it led to the bank president providing Adam with a tip for a story that Adam might not have stumbled upon for another few months. "It was a really, really good story that was of

Figure 5.6 This is another example of a house ad that *Harvey County Now* ran to promote Press Club. Courtesy of Kansas Publishing Ventures.

huge community interest," Adam said. "Those little connections here and there, you pick up this and that's been helpful."

Moving forward, Joey plans to increase the corporate sponsorship to $2,500 annually. Also, he and Bruce will adopt a more strategic approach to selling sponsorships, incorporating them into broader packages. "Bruce and I decided that it was smart for us to just stop trying to separate everything," Joey said.

> If Press Club is going to be about doing events and getting people together, let's make it that. Let's bring in Blues, Brews, & Barbecue. Let's do the mingles. You get to be a sponsor of it all. And it's a really compelling sponsorship package in a lot of ways. When you put it all together, it's like, man, the newspaper does a lot of stuff.

One important aspect of the Press Club approach is that discussions about potential sponsorships are just part of regular sales conversations. To put it differently, selling Press Club seamlessly integrates into Joey and Bruce's existing sales routines, without adding extra labor or time. "Press Club is a piece of my menu," Bruce said. "It's not the main course. It's a piece of my menu. So, when I'm visiting with a business, we'll talk about print, we'll talk about digital, we'll talk about several things, and Press Club is just one of those."

At the conclusion of the year-long experiment, there were 149 Press Club members at *Harvey County Now*. While Press Club had not yet launched in Hillsboro, and its structure will continue to change in Newton, it will remain an integral part of the team's operations. "It's kind of reclaiming some of that galvanizing the community type that people have really gravitated to," Joey said. "It's great to have our fans in a room together."

The Model: E-newsletters

E-newsletters interested the team at *Harvey County Now* even before the experiment year. However, the staff previously struggled to put the strategy into practice. During the April 2022 meeting with the researchers, Joey said they loved the idea, but "I wish we could figure out how to do it." "We've tried," Adam said. Lindsey said she signed up for a training webinar and was excited to learn more only to be overwhelmed by how much work the instructor made it seem. "You can put hours upon hours into each, you know, daily or weekly newsletter," she said.

> But are you getting that return the same way that you're getting it out of the newspaper or other revenue streams that you're planning? … It feels like it's just right outta reach for where we can figure out the most effective way to do it.

After Joey said he wished he could talk to someone who had been successful with e-newsletters to get help, the researchers reached out to Forum Communications, a multi-state media company based in Fargo, North Dakota. The company's e-newsletter team agreed to do a Zoom training for *Harvey County Now* for free to help with the experiment and get them up to speed on the e-newsletter software MailChimp.

Two months after the training, *Harvey County Now* reported significant progress with its e-newsletter. Joey said they changed the name, added more visuals, changed colors, and assigned Adam to be in charge to curate content and analyze what gets engagement. Adam said these basic changes immediately brought a 5–10% increase in open rates from the existing audience even before they began additional sign-up recruitment. He said studying which topics get the most clicks helped liven up the newsletter, with their community most interested in business, obits, and crime. When asked in June 2022 if there were discussions about selling ads in the e-newsletter, Bruce said he didn't think they were there yet. "I want to see what the click-through rate would be, you know," he said. "I just don't quite think I'm at my comfort level yet, but we're pretty damn close." Joey said they were trying to be intentional about making the newsletter good first so that they can show engagement statistics to advertisers. The team also began development of a second newsletter just for Press Club members that featured upcoming activities.

During a staff meeting in early August 2022, Tommy reported a significant increase in the number of people on the website on Thursdays after the e-newsletter came out. All of the e-newsletter content has a paywall and is therefore only visible to paying subscribers of the newspaper. Joey wanted to add a pop-up on the website to get more people to sign up for the newsletter. Adam noted that Facebook is purposefully not putting their social media posts in front of people, thereby making him feel positive about the importance and future of the e-newsletter. "This is a really good system to develop so you make sure that you are relevant and getting news in people's feeds," Adam said of the e-newsletter. "I think that this is a way of us preparing post-social media 'cause I think there will be a post-social media point where we can't use social media as a part of our business model."

Nine months into the increased emphasis on e-newsletters, Adam was even more sold on the concept. In an emailed exchange with the researchers in March 2023, he said e-newsletters were "the easiest and best solution rural newspapers can implement to maintain readership, grow it, or transition it" as older subscribers are gradually replaced by younger ones. *Harvey County Now* had increased to publishing three newsletters a week and saw an increase in engagement as people got into the habit of more frequent interaction with local news. Just as useful, the newspaper saw nearly 70 people click to subscribe to the newspaper through the e-newsletter. Subscriptions as a whole remained stable even with the e-newsletter, while web traffic jumped significantly. "Facebook has all but shut down any hard news we post, and this has been a great way to get important issues out between publication days," Adam said. "This has been a case study for us on why newsletters work."

After the year-long experiment concluded, the staff universally hailed e-newsletters as the most impactful aspect of what they tried. "All the feedback we've gotten on the e-newsletter has been universally good," Joey said. "I would argue it's maybe the most successful thing we've done. It's definitely the thing that I get the most comments about from just regular readers." Over the course of the year, they built the e-newsletter listserv to approximately 3,000 subscribers, or a 15% increase. "That's been our main success of the year, and, to me, I'd argue our main success of the program," Adam said. "Yes, we are bringing in more finances through Press Club, but, to me, the most useful thing is the e-newsletter." Joey takes no credit for the success of the e-newsletter, directing praise to Adam, who has shepherded the product since its inception. "The only thing I've done is said, 'Adam, go get it.' And he has," Joey said.

"Adam developed it. Adam takes care of it. Adam maintains it. Adam curates it. He does everything. It is his baby. He absolutely obsesses over it."

While a staff member does not necessarily need to "obsess" over the product, it does require someone to take ownership. Adam said:

> I have made it a priority, and I think if you're going to have a successful newsletter or get a big benefit from it, you have to prioritize it, just like you prioritize the print product or what you're trying to do online.

Initially, admittedly, Adam spent too much time on the e-newsletter. He tinkered with the template, put in extra work on headlines, and inserted numerous links. These additions proved to be a subtraction. "It did worse," Adam said,

> I spent more time on it, and it did less. So, now ours is just like something where I could just sit at the end of the day and just be like, boom, boom, boom, and then I can move on.

Joey observed the efficiency of the e-newsletter system when Adam took a week of vacation. "I got one out in, like, 15 minutes, and it really didn't take very much time," Joey said.

> It was real slick. It's really not that hard. It's hard to screw it up. … Through Adam, I will say that what I've learned is that consistency is really important. Simple is better than complicated. The news is what people want, so that's what you should give them.

The team noticed three tangible benefits from the e-newsletter over the year. First, it bolstered revenue. Since subscribing to the newspaper is a prerequisite for reading the e-newsletter, it led to readers subscribing. Initially apprehensive like many publishers, Joey's concerns about the e-newsletter overshadowing the weekly printed product proved wrong. "I don't think that's a founded fear now that we've been doing this for a year," Joey said. Furthermore, Bruce successfully secured a sponsor for the e-newsletter. "I am officially shocked by that," Joey said. The initial $250 price tag was almost immediately deemed too low, prompting plans for a price increase, aligning it with the premium position they believe it holds. "I honestly think that number is going to double, maybe triple," Joey said. "It's a premium upsell." He explained that the printed newspaper rarely displays above-the-fold ads on the front page. "I want to say, maybe a dozen times in eight years," Joey said.

> But we sell it for just a ridiculous amount of money because we see that as the most prime real estate we have, and we don't devalue it. … I think as Adam really grows the e-newsletter, (that ad position) is going to become our digital equivalent.

Second, an internal benefit to the e-newsletters emerged – an enthusiastic participation from the reporting team. “I didn’t realize (the e-newsletter) would be such a benefit to the newsroom and my life,” Joey said.

> When you’re a weekly, (reporters) write on deadline; they all do. Because we put out this newsletter over five times a week, and we tell reporters, “You better be writing all week, so we have fresh stuff to put in it,” they write every day. They don’t wait until Tuesday to write all of their stuff. They write every day. It’s amazing.

This shift proved transformative. “Everyone’s bought in,” Adam said. “Everybody wants to be in the newsletter now. So, it’s kind of motivated people to get stuff done regularly.”

The third benefit was external, a shift of audience perception of their news organization. “I think it’s made people that maybe were not pumped about us ‘just being a weekly’ to now it’s like, ‘Oh, we feel like you are more like a daily,’” Lindsey said. Joey concurred, emphasizing the perceptive shift in identity. “We always said that we were a weekly in print, but we were a daily online,” Joey said.

> This (e-newsletter) actually makes it feel like we’re a daily online because we are actually producing a newsletter and sending news when it’s done to readers’ inboxes at least four times a week. … Perception is reality. And if you’re a weekly newspaper, people think you’re a weekly newspaper, you come out weekly. (The e-newsletter is) a perception of value I think for readers. It’s something that we can say, “Hey, like this is something else that we’re doing that we’re trying to improve your local news experience.”

The success of the e-newsletter even prompted the team to reconsider a potential future of *Harvey County News,* envisioning a complete shift away from the printed product. “Adam is convinced to this day that if they ever price us out of printing the paper that we can move to a newsletter style delivery system and that could be the future of *Harvey County Now*,” Joey said.

The Model: Events

In addition to the Press Club monthly mingles, *Harvey County Now* explored adding other events for club members. Five years prior, the newspaper created a Blues, Brews & Barbecue event that attracts about 1,000 people each September in Newton. The event brings in bands, craft beer vendors, and food trucks, generating a few thousand dollars in profit for *Harvey County Now* each year. Beyond the money, Adam said the effort also illustrates that the newspaper is community focused and trying to make the town better.

In June 2022, Lindsey was looking forward to exploring more event options that the newspaper could host. "I think anything that can help us be more part of the community and fill gaps in the community and just become more involved is gonna be a really interesting way for us to interact," she said. "If you look into the history of how communities used to function, the newspaper was, like, the hub, and I think we can continue to be that now."

One of the team's initial new event ideas was to partner with an area brewery and host a field trip for a behind-the-scenes tour, with a goal to host one field trip each quarter. The group also brainstormed the possibility of hosting poker nights, book clubs, and art nights. One small activity that *Harvey County Now* launched early was monthly dinners for club members at local restaurants. Joey said they called the restaurant in advance to let them know how many club members signed up through the website to make sure the eatery was prepared so that everyone had a good experience. Similarly, club members were invited to come to trivia nights at the local bar.

The researchers of this book also worked with the newspaper staff to host informal audience focus group events in both Newton and Hillsboro in June and September 2022, respectively, to explain the business model experiment to about a dozen community members in each city. The gatherings also provided a chance for residents to provide feedback about the newspapers. Wanting to keep these sessions informal for rural residents unaccustomed to academic research, the researchers did not formally record data. However, residents were asked what they value about their local newspaper, what content they liked best, what content would improve the paper, their willingness to pay for news, and their thoughts on memberships, e-newsletters, and events. While residents in Newton were positive about the newspaper, it quickly became clear that Hillsboro was more critical and wanted to see improvements in coverage. The constructive feedback initially rattled the staff, but Joey said he was glad they did the focus group events in both communities. "If we wouldn't have done the in-person focus group in Hillsboro, we would have launched the wrong thing," he said of their initial plan to do an NPR-style funding campaign,

> It was really informative of maybe some of the faults the paper has and some of the things that we maybe need to start playing with. I've had a lot of people tell me they're like, "You should do an in-person focus group more often," and we've never done it, and I get why people don't do it because some of the stuff you hear is not always easy to hear. But if they show up to an in-person focus group, they probably have some buy-in … [newspapers should] really take it in and try to do something with that feedback.

The biggest challenge the team faced during the entire year-long experiment was undoubtedly gaining traction in Hillsboro, whether through Press Club or through other events. Conversations with city officials about potential events began as early as fall 2022, gradually paving the way for the organization of a barbecue competition. Joey attributed this challenge to a clear factor. "I don't live in Hillsboro," he said.

> I think it's really important if you own a group (of newspapers) to meet people where they are and talk to them about what they want, especially if you don't live in their community. They see you as an outsider. … I live 20 minutes from Hillsboro. I'm as local as they are going to get, but I'm still an outsider. I don't live in town. And rather than feel slighted by that designation, just meet them where they are.

Listening to the residents, either in focus groups or informal daily interactions, is the key, Joey said. "I've always said that the newspaper publisher or editor in a community is the most informed person in town," he said.

> So, you are the most informed person to know exactly what your community needs. What are people going out of town for? Can you bring it to them for one night? Can you figure out how to bring a little bit of entertainment, if that's what it is?

Accordingly, potential changes to the business model in Hillsboro were still pending by the end of the experiment time even as they flourished in Newton.

During the latter half of the experiment year in Newton, the team orchestrated its most successful non-mingle event – a field trip to a suite at the Wichita minor-league baseball team, attended by 25 Press Club members. Such successes, along with the annual Blues, Brews & Barbecue event, led Joey to want to host four big events throughout the year. "We might start doing more than that," Joey said, "but, in the next year, our goal is to do four events." As time progresses, the planning for these events will become easier and increasingly streamlined. "The Year 2 of Press Club, I think it'll be so much easier for us to organize stuff," Joey said. "One of the reasons we were able to organize that thing (at the brewery) is that I'm friends with all the ownership group. They were like, 'The newspaper's doing what?' … But they trusted me." Lindsey envisions that, over time, the news organization will build a reputation for uniting the community. "It has just been such a neat way to interact with our community in a different way," Lindsey said of the events. Perhaps most important to the continued momentum and sustained success of events is Joey's genuine enjoyment of them:

> You're probably going to ask me how much time I spent on (Press Club and events) and sometimes I don't even really notice. This is one of the fun things I get to do. Organizing mingles and setting up a ballgame doesn't feel like a lot of work. It's like, oh, you mean, I get to go sit in a box seat at the ballgame in Wichita with 25 people from Newton? I mean, what part of that is a bunch of work? Like, it doesn't feel like a lot of work. That just seems like something fun to do.

Reflecting on the Experiment

The year-long experiment chronicled in this chapter brought, to some extent, Joey and Lindsey into the spotlight, garnering invitations to speak at numerous state press associations and similar events across the country. Not fans of flying, they crisscrossed the country by car. Throughout their journeys, they ventured through small town after small town, keeping a close eye out for newspapers just like their own. "Joey and I have been traveling a lot," Lindsey said. "There are a lot of communities that look very much like Newton." Lindsey firmly believes that many of the towns, along with their community news organizations, have the potential to emulate the success in Newton with *Harvey County Now.* "I would be a liar if I said I thought this would work at every single newspaper, but I do think that this works at a lot of newspapers," Lindsey said. Adam agreed, emphasizing an important caveat. "I think it would depend on their community."

A telling example lies in the contrasting approaches of Kansas Publishing Ventures toward Newton and Hillsboro during the year-long experiment. Living in Newton, working in Newton, and being deeply embedded in the community of Newton, they understood the nuances of the town. This knowledge empowered them to forge ahead full-steam, seamlessly integrating memberships, events, and e-newsletters into their newsroom repertoire. In Hillsboro, however, they encountered stumbling blocks. They were humbled by criticisms of being perceived as "outsiders," despite living just 25 miles away. While they found almost immediate success in Newton during this experiment, progress in Hillsboro took measured steps that only materialized toward the end of the year. These steps included discussions of organizing a small event and considering modest gestures, such as distributing T-shirts and coffee mugs to Press Club members. "We could have launched in Hillsboro faster, but I don't think it would have been helpful," Joey said. Initially, the intention was to replicate the additions made in Newton in Hillsboro. "My original plan for Hillsboro would have failed," he said. The stark contrast in their experiences between Newton and Hillsboro drove home the crucial lesson that a deep understanding of a community's needs, desires, and dynamics is paramount. "Look at ways to find those gaps (in the community)," Adam said. "I think that the two parts of it would be finding that gap and doing something to fill that gap. For us, (in Newton), it was social events in the evening."

As the year-long experiment ended, the leaders at Kansas Publishing Ventures were asked to reflect on their experiences and offer guidance to their peers across the country. As noted, first and most important is to deeply understand the community, actively listening to residents, and addressing their needs and wants. Following that, it is crucial to fully understand your business, evaluating it critically and creatively from all angles. "I think that it was incredibly beneficial that we started looking at the entire business holistically and really paying a little more attention to additional revenue streams and how we are doing stuff," Adam said. "I don't think this was a moment too soon.

The pressures on local publications have increased immensely." The Kansas Publishing Ventures leaders believe they have taken the essential measures to secure a more promising future. "While we are in a really challenging time right now," Adam said, "I find that I think we're a little better off than a lot of our peers across the state."

Joey's advice to fellow owners and publishers is clear-cut: Do not let fear be a barrier. "I think they need to get over fear," he said.

> What I would do is start small. … Experiment small, grow into it. Every publisher I talk to, fear is such a big driver of why they do things or how they operate. And until they can get over some of the fear, it's going to be a struggle. So, the best way to get over that fear, dip your toe in.

Some publishers who will read this chapter may be tempted to emulate every facet of Kansas Publishing Ventures' innovations. If publishers are not comfortable with a full-scale approach, Joey advises them to consider adopting *some* aspect, or even explore their own innovations. "Some people just dive into the deep end," Joey said. "It's like, 'Hey, you know what, that's cold water. We're just gonna get over it. The shock will eventually go away.' That's how I'm geared." Lindsey, on the other hand, has a different approach.

> Lindsey is a, "I'm gonna put my foot in, and then I'm gonna put my second foot in, and then I'm gonna take a step into the water." She just kinda eases her way in. And I would say that if that's your approach, then do that with the business. … Experiment small, ease your way in. Let it prove to you that this works or doesn't work. I don't know. But figure it out. It's better to do something than nothing.

Lindsey's advice is to start close to home, engaging with friends and avid supporters of the paper. "The guy that every time you're just selling a random ad for a random page is just like, 'Yeah, just sign me up.' Those are the people to start with," she said. Those are the individuals who will, in turn, become valuable contributors to the news organization, acting as enthusiastic advocates and attracting others to join the organization's initiatives. "The movers and shakers in the community, they are gonna be the ones, the extroverts, who are gonna grab their buddies and say, 'Come on. We're gonna do this cool thing.'"

Beyond revenue, beyond innovation, beyond security, Kansas Publishing Ventures' most substantial gain from the year-long endeavor was a stronger connection to their community. "It humanizes us," Bruce said. "I think it's just given us more of a face," Lindsey said. "I think it's made us a little more approachable and given us more humanity than maybe we would have otherwise." The mingles, where they share laughs, drinks, and stories with residents, especially highlight this. "Adam's not the scary journalist from the newspaper that they've only had like four conversations with – because now they've had conversations with him a lot," Joey said. These connections make the job easier for Adam, and all reporters, too. "It makes when you are wanting to ask questions easier because you've got a personal rapport," Joey said. At the mingles and events, residents see the Kansas Publishing Ventures employees as people, not as journalists. "We're engaging people in a way that shows some personality, shows that we're just like them," Joey said. "We're neighbors. We're people who live in the community. That's been really valuable on a long-term scale."

A prime illustration of the year's success is Joey's connection with the head of the county's Republican Party. Joey openly acknowledges that he and the official "do not agree on a lot of things." Nevertheless, the official consistently attends almost every newspaper gathering and was among the initial members to join the Press Club. "He goes to bat for the newspaper all the time," Joey said of the official. "He always just says, 'Have you gone and talked to them? If you go to talk to them, they're reasonable human beings. They'll listen to you.' He says that all the time. I've heard him say it." Such support exemplifies the power of dialogue, respect, and connection, transcending differences in opinion. "He clearly likes the paper, he likes us, and he feels that we're reasonable," Joey said. "In my opinion, that's a huge win." While the year-long experiment – the Press Club, events, and e-newsletters – provided short-term financial gains, it is these enduring personal connections that hold immeasurable value, forming the foundation for long-term success for Kansas Publishing Ventures.

6 Rural Journalism and Disruption

Nick Mathews and Patrick Ferrucci

In May 2023, the four members of the Kansas Publishing Ventures ownership team met around a patio table on the screened-in porch at Adam Strunk's house. Joey and Lindsey Young, alongside Bruce Behymer, gathered for their customary monthly meeting. However, it was, as Bruce described it, "a speak now or forever hold your peace." The day's topic: The future of their business. Seated together, they scrutinized their finances, acknowledging the challenges ahead and the inability to maintain the status quo. Joey's question lingered a bit: "What are we going to do?"

The four leaders found themselves willing to consider change because of the groundwork laid over the preceding year implementing its Press Club model of memberships, e-newsletters, and events. As the year progressed, the accumulation of mingles, conversations, and relationship-building led the four leaders to gain an improved understanding of their community and their organization's place within it. "It's been fun to actually just see that we have some fans in the community," Lindsey said. This newfound understanding armed them with the strength to provide a surprising answer to Joey's question about their future – to significantly raise the subscription rate for *Harvey County Now* and make all subscribers part of the Press Club membership program. The decision to change the rate from $66 per year to $144 per year defied conventions embraced by the newspaper industry to either never change or barely change subscription prices. Without the preceding year, without Press Club, such a decision would have been impossible. "I think that we would have been too scared to do that," Lindsey said. "But we've seen just how supportive our community is of us and how much people really do care about what we do. Through a lot of this, I think it gave us a little bit more bravery to move forward."

"We all agreed that raising the prices gave us anxiety," Joey said. "Every single one of us universally said, 'This makes me anxious.'" On that May porch summit, they considered other options, beyond just increasing the subscription. One common approach used in newsrooms across the country was to cut expenses. "After we talked about that," Adam said, "it was like, 'Look, I don't want to just die by 1,000 cuts.'" The option of eliminating personnel

DOI: 10.4324/9781003414582-6

was never really an option. "We don't want to be in this business if we can't pay a fair wage with benefits," Joey said.

> We don't want to cut our newsroom to a bone. We're not willing to do what Gannett, and GateHouse, and all these (corporate) groups are willing to do, which is just cut journalists. We don't want to do that. … We aren't going to run that newspaper.

They meticulously analyzed their finances, scrutinizing payroll expenses, benefits, paper costs, mail expenses, and other factors to establish a baseline rate. Adam posted the pivotal question: "What does it cost us to produce one paper?" The answer they arrived at was $3.03 per issue. "Our average subscriber was paying like $1.29 (per issue)," Joey said. "It's completely unsustainable." Put another way, as Adam said, "It made us feel really dumb." Their decision to increase the subscription price and make everyone a Press Club member was not only driven by their thorough organization-specific financial assessment but also aligned with the challenges faced by the news industry overall. "Everybody's paper costs are up. Everybody's postage is up," Joey said.

> It is more expensive and harder to find (staff members) than it ever has been in the history of the newspaper industry. Harder to find people, and it's more expensive when you do. Nothing is easy right now. Nothing. Whether you're big, you're small, it doesn't matter, family owned, corporately owned. Nothing's easy. So, our solution to that is, it's better to try something than to sit back and take it.

The consensus solidified at the porch summit, with Joey stating, "We all agreed."

On June 8, 2023, they published a front-page, centerpiece article "The cost to print." The sub-headline read: "Skyrocketing prices nationwide forcing change with *Harvey County Now*" (Figure 6.1). The article presented the intricate details of the industry, pointing to such things as the 50% surge in mailing costs over the past two years. Joey and Lindsey also revealed their total annual compensation, with Joey stating in the story, "Lindsey and I only take $47,500 combined out of the company a year." Lindsey said:

> We talked about how comfortable we felt with that. Was that something that we felt was important to include? And the two of us kind of determined that, "Yeah." We know that there are so many big corporations in this country where the CEO is making tons and tons of money while everybody's getting laid off at the bottom. And we didn't want our community to have any question about where we were at, that Joey and I were not these greedy, top-heavy CEO types.

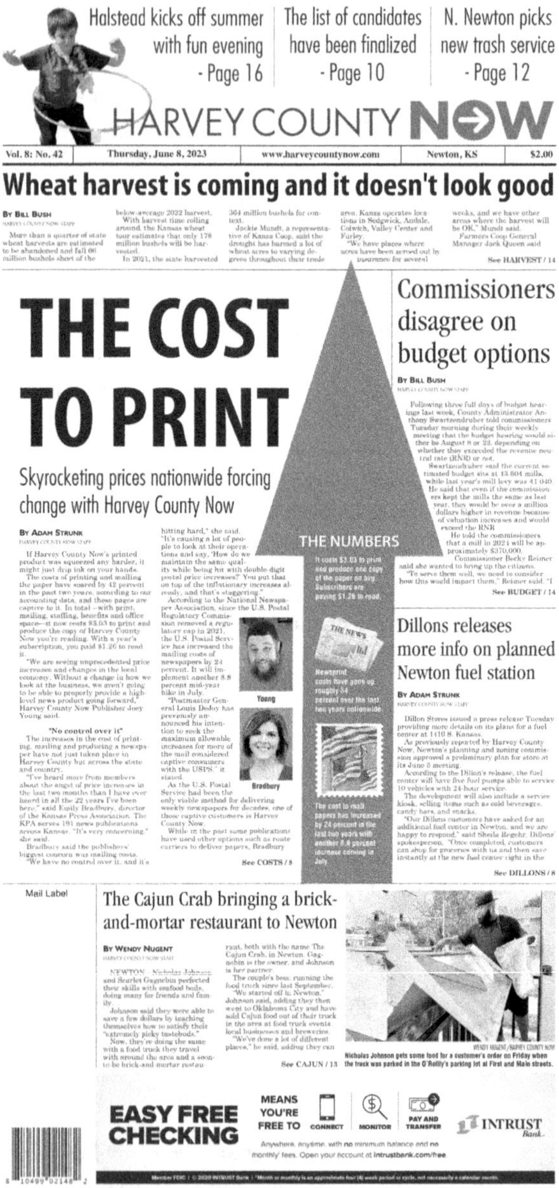

Halstead kicks off summer with fun evening - Page 16

The list of candidates have been finalized - Page 10

N. Newton picks new trash service - Page 12

HARVEY COUNTY NOW

Vol. 8: No. 42	Thursday, June 8, 2023	www.harveycountynow.com	Newton, KS	$2.00

Wheat harvest is coming and it doesn't look good

BY BILL BUSH
HARVEY COUNTY NOW STAFF

More than a quarter of state wheat harvests are estimated to be abandoned and fall 66 million bushels short of the below-average 2022 harvest.

With harvest time rolling around, the Kansas wheat tour estimates that only 178 million bushels will be harvested.

In 2021, the state harvested 364 million bushels for context.

Jackie Mundt, a representative of Kanza Coop, said the drought has harmed a lot of wheat acres to varying degrees throughout their trade area. Kanza operates locations in Sedgwick, Andale, Colwich, Valley Center and Furley.

"We have places where acres have been zeroed out by insurance for several weeks, and we have other areas where the harvest will be OK," Mundt said.

Farmers Coop General Manager Jack Queen said

See HARVEST / 14

THE COST TO PRINT

Skyrocketing prices nationwide forcing change with Harvey County Now

BY ADAM STRUNK
HARVEY COUNTY NOW STAFF

If Harvey County Now's printed product was squeezed any harder, it might just drip ink on your hands.

The costs of printing and mailing the paper have soared by 42 percent in the past two years, according to our accounting data, and these pages are captive to it. In total – with print, mailing, staffing, benefits and office space—it now costs $3.03 to print and produce the copy of Harvey County Now you're reading. With a year's subscription, you paid $1.26 to read it.

"We are seeing unprecedented price increases and changes in the local economy. Without a change in how we look at the business, we aren't going to be able to properly provide a high-level news product going forward," Harvey County Now Publisher Joey Young said.

"No control over it"

The increases in the cost of printing, mailing and producing a newspaper have not just taken place in Harvey County but across the state and country.

"I've heard more from members about the angst of price increases in the last two months than I have ever heard in all the 22 years I've been here," said Emily Bradbury, director of the Kansas Press Association. The KPA serves 191 news publications across Kansas. "It's very concerning," she said.

Bradbury said the publishers' biggest concern was mailing costs.

"We have no control over it, and it's hitting hard," she said. "It's causing a lot of people to look at their operations and say, 'How do we maintain the same quality while being hit with double-digit postal price increases?' You put that on top of the inflationary increases already, and that's staggering."

According to the National Newspaper Association, since the U.S. Postal Regulatory Commission removed a regulatory cap in 2021, the U.S. Postal Service has increased the mailing costs of newspapers by 24 percent. It will implement another 8.8 percent mid-year hike in July.

Young

Bradbury

"Postmaster General Louis DeJoy has previously announced his intention to seek the maximum allowable increases for more of the mail considered captive consumers with the USPS," it stated.

As the U.S. Postal Service had been the only viable method for delivering weekly newspapers for decades, one of those captive customers is Harvey County Now.

While in the past some publications have used other options such as route carriers to deliver papers, Bradbury

See COSTS / 8

THE NUMBERS

It costs $3.03 to print and produce one copy of the paper on avg. Subscribers are paying $1.26 to read.

Newsprint costs have gone up roughly 84 percent over the last two years nationwide.

The cost to mail papers has increased by 24 percent in the last two years with another 8.8 percent increase coming in July.

Commissioners disagree on budget options

BY BILL BUSH
HARVEY COUNTY NOW STAFF

Following three full days of budget hearings last week, County Administrator Anthony Swartzendruber told commissioners Tuesday morning during their weekly meeting that the budget hearing would either be August 8 or 22, depending on whether they exceeded the revenue neutral rate (RNR) or not.

Swartzendruber said the current estimated budget sits at 43.604 mills, while last year's mill levy was 41.040. He said that even if the commissioners kept the mills the same as last year, they would be over a million dollars higher in revenue because of valuation increases and would exceed the RNR.

He told the commissioners that a mill in 2024 will be approximately $370,000.

Commissioner Becky Reimer said she wanted to bring up the citizens.

"To serve them well, we need to consider how this would impact them," Reimer said. "I

See BUDGET / 14

Dillons releases more info on planned Newton fuel station

BY ADAM STRUNK
HARVEY COUNTY NOW STAFF

Dillon Stores issued a press release Tuesday providing more details on its plans for a fuel center at 1410 S. Kansas.

As previously reported by Harvey County Now, Newton's planning and zoning commission approved a preliminary plan for store at its June 5 meeting.

According to the Dillon's release, the fuel center will have five fuel pumps able to service 10 vehicles with 24-hour service.

The development will also include a service kiosk, selling items such as cold beverages, candy bars, and snacks.

"Our Dillons customers have asked for an additional fuel center in Newton, and we are happy to respond," said Sheila Regehr, Dillons' spokesperson. "Once completed, customers can shop for groceries with us and then save instantly at the new fuel center right in the

See DILLONS / 8

Mail Label

The Cajun Crab bringing a brick-and-mortar restaurant to Newton

BY WENDY NUGENT
HARVEY COUNTY NOW STAFF

NEWTON – Nicholas Johnson and Scarlet Gagnebin perfected their skills with seafood boils, doing many for friends and family.

Johnson said they were able to save a few dollars by teaching themselves how to satisfy their "extremely picky tastebuds."

Now, they're doing the same with a food truck they travel with around the area and a soon-to-be brick-and-mortar restaurant, both with the name The Cajun Crab, in Newton. Gagnebin is the owner, and Johnson is her partner.

The couple's been running the food truck since last September.

"We started off in Newton," Johnson said, adding they then went to Oklahoma City and have sold Cajun food out of their truck in the area at food truck events, local businesses and breweries.

"We've done a lot of different places," he said, adding they can

See CAJUN / 13

WENDY NUGENT/HARVEY COUNTY NOW

Nicholas Johnson gets some food for a customer's order on Friday when the truck was parked in the O'Reilly's parking lot at First and Main streets.

EASY FREE CHECKING MEANS YOU'RE FREE TO CONNECT MONITOR PAY AND TRANSFER

INTRUST Bank

Anywhere, anytime, with no minimum balance and no monthly fees. Open your account at intrustbank.com/free.

8 10499 02148 2

Figure 6.1 *Harvey County Now* ran a front-page centerpiece story on June 8, 2023, giving readers a complete picture of the newspaper's finances and why subscription rates would increase. The newspaper found it cost $3.03 to print one newspaper but subscribers were paying $1.29. Courtesy of Kansas Publishing Ventures.

The month between the May porch summit and the June publication of the story was fraught with tension. "I'm not going to lie," Lindsey said,

> It definitely gave me a pit in my stomach, all the way up until it was on the page. … It was not an easy decision at all. I think Adam put off writing it for at least an extra week just because he also was really nervous about it.

Joey explained more:

> We demand transparency from government. Shouldn't people demand transparency from who gives them the coverage on the government? If you're not honest with your readers about what's going on in your business, how do you expect them to trust you on what's going on in the government's business? If you can't be honest about what's going on in the industry and with your newspaper, with your readers, you can't look at the mayor and say, "Why'd you lie about this?" … It is everything we believe in journalistically to be honest with your readers. And that includes your business.

They acknowledged the potential for readers to rebuff the new subscription price, resulting in substantial losses in revenue or even the closure of the newspaper. But Joey was confident in the transparent approach:

> If you just are honest with your readers, and you say, "This is what we need to stay to be solvent going forward – this is the business plan going forward," I truly believe your readers are going to respond favorably to that. And we believe very, very strongly that a high, big majority of our readers are going to re-up at the higher rate.

For many news organizations, making such a seismic change without the prior groundwork of a year of transparency could inevitably result in exactly what Kansas Publishing Ventures feared: closure. However, three months after announcing to readers the higher cost of the newspaper, Lindsey reported only a 4% decline in subscriptions while making double the revenue from the other 96%. The disruptive innovation of the prior year had been a success.

Rural Journalism and Disruption

When scholars research the intersection of journalism and disruption, the main focus, understandably, is often something concerning technology, particularly digital technology. This makes sense as it should come as no surprise to anyone reading this book – or anything in this book series – that digital technologies have significantly impacted the journalism ecosystem globally, in both positive and negative manners. However, when Christensen (2013) explicated his theory of disruptive innovation, he carefully noted that innovation does not always equate to technological innovation, despite its primacy in the disruption of virtually all occupations and organizations in the 21st century. In fact, according to the theory, technology itself is "the processes by which an organization transforms labor, capital, materials, and information into products and services of greater value" (Christensen, 2013, p. xvi). The clear takeaway is that technology can mean processes that are both digital and analog in nature, something that does not definitively include something tangible. Therefore, the adoption of a new business model for a journalism organization, a process whereby a newsroom would transform labor, capital, and other elements into something of greater value to the organization, would absolutely qualify as both disruptive, innovative, and technological.

While all industries today seem to casually throw around buzzwords such as innovation and disruption as hackneyed signifiers of some potential economic panacea (Ferrucci, 2018), the journalism industry, since the beginnings of its severe economic crises in the early 21st century, has done this as much or more than others (Gynnild, 2014; Lewis & Usher, 2013). But the journalism industry, from an economic standpoint, essentially slept frozen in carbonite for almost 100 years; the industry's advertising-funded model and deeply entrenched normative processes effectively made the profession stable and similar across all organizations (Ferrucci & Kuhn, 2022). Therefore, across the United States, for roughly the entire 20th century, organizations structured themselves in ways – in terms of both people and processes – that served the model.

Stinchcombe (1965) argued that organizational change is not simply a unilateral process, something that can be accomplished the same way in any instance. He specifically noted that when effectually ossified organizations such as those in journalism that have been entrenched in the same model of doing business attempt to innovate, they are often not successful. This was dubbed the liability of newness, the idea that for an older organization to embrace disruptive innovation, it basically needs to become a new organization. Other scholars have labeled the ability to embrace disruption as organizational agility, which, if an organization possesses it, "enables an organization to adapt to volatile and unforeseen business scenarios through resource reconfiguration, both via integration of internal and external capability" (Ganguly et al., 2022, p. 1). The lack of organizational agility can easily be seen in the journalism field, a profession that saw advertising revenues shrink, but had no ability to adapt to a new funding structure. This is due to the entire operation being undergirded by advertising in multiple manners: space in news print based on advertising sales; organizational members employed solely to sell advertising; low subscription costs aimed entirely at boosting circulation numbers to increase advertising revenue; norms revolving around mitigating advertising influence on editorial practice; a mission-driven approach initially offering content freely online where digital advertising rates paled in comparison to print; etc. (Ferrucci & Perreault, 2022).

Before the experiment detailed in this book began, as previously noted, the authors conducted focus groups with rural newspaper publishers (detailed in Chapter 3). A main goal of these meetings revolved around the researchers attempting to understand publishers' perceptions concerning innovation, particularly about revenue streams. It became clear, almost immediately, that these publishers did not favor even a little innovation. Repeatedly, a publisher shared something like the following paraphrased message: "This is what we are and I'd rather close up shop than change." It took roughly five minutes to realize that despite the overwhelmingly precarious economic futures faced by these news organizations, the publishers did not really desire to change in basically any way.

There are a lot of very good reasons for this. First, and most notably, these publishers readily admitted that they knew their newsrooms faced a tremendously negative financial outlook; these newsrooms, many of them, were barely hanging on. Change, or innovation, necessitates resources, both monetarily and with people/time. To adopt a new model would be a gamble that would need some form of resource buy-in, and if the innovation did not yield the desired result, it very well could be the determining factor that caused the newsroom's closure. Second, many of these publishers had owned these newsrooms for extended periods of time; some of the newspapers had been in the publishers' families for generations. So again, simply telling these publishers to innovate might seem simple enough, but these are operations with processes that have stayed the same for decades or more. To simply change would require a basically new organizational infrastructure; thus, these newsrooms had little perceived organizational agility despite often being under local control instead of corporately owned. Or, in other words, the humans at the center of these organizations lack the agility needed to successfully implement change (Crocitto & Youssef, 2003). Third, the perception that newspapers are a business and civic service, at the same time, also became clear during these focus groups. These publishers believed that the historic business model of journalism, combined with the normative practices undertaken by journalists, is what makes journalism actually journalism.

Taken together, it seems obvious why rural newspaper publishers perceived change as something untenable. When looking at the manner in which they ran their businesses, it felt clear that any kind of funding model innovation not only carried inexcusable risk, but it also seemed highly unlikely to succeed due to infrastructure and fear of deviating from the normative foundation of the practice; in sum, these collective perceptions would absolutely hinder any notion of innovation (Barrett et al., 2015). This perception, however, particularly in the case of journalism, should not be accepted.

We argue this because our reader surveys clearly indicated a major disconnect between modern consumers and an industry still operating under a model developed in the 1800s. While the newsroom historically has psychologically maintained an invisible wall between the financial and editorial sides of a newspaper, the fact of the matter is this is still a business. Even putting that aside, the industry's longtime pride in providing a service to communities needs to be reevaluated if consumers don't feel like they are being well served by the current product. The academic theory grounding this work – the push to incorporate memberships, e-newsletters, and events into rural weeklies – came directly from rural readers themselves. The fact that these respondents frequently noted they wanted news more often and more news provided to them illustrates that local news is indeed still viewed as important. Yet the news industry isn't providing sufficient avenues to capitalize on reader revenue as it instead continues to grasp onto a centuries-old (failing) advertising model that has, we argue, falsely become equated with "objectivity" and the definition of journalism. It is actually a pretty straightforward proposition: Readers overwhelmingly reiterated the desire for more news and more engagement with their news organization. Yet, as mentioned, publishers seemingly hoped to ignore this want, happy to keep doing what they had always done, just with a lesser product, all the while surprised at lackluster economic returns.

Notably, this research also busted the myth that only senior citizens are invested in local news and that younger readers are not worth the energy of newspapers. Quite contrarily, our survey found Millennials and Generation Z were more likely to say they would financially help their newspaper than boomers were. In practice, Press Club attendance at *Harvey County Now* events came strongly from millennials. While not every news organization may have the manpower to do monthly events like *Harvey County Now*, editors and publishers should consider how a membership program could work in their community. Even a quarterly speaker program of interest to community members could be a simple start. As we have toured the country in the past year introducing this concept of business model innovation, it is clear it will be a long road getting the industry to change, however. Even as thousands of newspapers die around them, many publishers are determined to cling to the status quo and resist innovation that could ensure their survival. The consequences of this are immense.

As noted throughout this book, rural journalism plays a large role in the very essence of community. In fact, the loss of rural journalism in a community would inevitably lead "to diminished democracy" since journalism "strengthens the overall ties of a community, which is a fundamental tenant of a strong democracy" (Ferrucci & Alaimo, 2020, p. 502). Earlier in this conclusion, it was noted that when describing the upcoming subscription price increase to readers, Kansas Publishing Ventures aimed to make it clear that, if their newspaper closes, "The truth is your taxes are going to go up. The truth is, you're going to be less informed. The truth is, you're going to have fewer candidates on the ballot. That is universally true." The majority of academic and professional research on the subject agrees: Living in an area without a dedicated news outlet results in positive effects for only folks committing nefarious acts (Matherly & Greenwood, 2021). But more than just taxes, more than corruption, the loss of news results in a loss of community ties and engagement (Griffin, 2018). This is why, at the end of her report, Abernathy (2018) called for some exploration into new funding structures of news; without them, more and more communities will face corruption and a loss of community, the kind of diminished democracy that Skocpol (2003) warned occurs in areas with a loss of civic institutions such as journalism organizations.

This dire potential outcome is exactly why the publishers that took part in this book's focus groups are so very wrong. Yes, change is difficult and, perhaps, could lead to another newspaper closure. But what is the alternative? Existing for a couple more years and then closing up shop? These publishers, while business owners, also have a civic obligation to their communities, an obligation to do whatever necessary in the fight for sustainability. Numerous studies surveying the professional identity of journalists find that a core belief of practitioners is that they serve the public as representatives, that the profession requires a commitment to the public before anything else (Deuze, 2008; Voakes, 1999). Publishers are the custodians of these civic enterprises, and they have the same responsibility to put the community and public first.

The Final Words

If anything, this book has demonstrated to business leaders that remaining complacent, stagnant, or passive in the news industry is not an option. It demands making changes, even bold ones, to not only survive but thrive. Bruce is beyond frustrated when he looks at the national news landscape and sees other industry leaders not taking the decisive actions exhibited by Kansas Publishing Ventures. "If I just had the time machine, I would go back and I would beat some business sense into newspaper people's hands," Bruce said, "and help them to understand that this is a business. If it's working, great, (still) do more, do better. If it's not (working), you're losing money. Either fix it or get out." The intensity of Bruce's emotions grew as he became even more animated about other publishers' idleness. "It gets me fired up," he said. "You've been doing the same thing over and over and over, and you're losing money, and you're skipping your pay periods and you're freaking out. Well, God damnit, fix it."

To be sure, Kansas Publishing Ventures is at the forefront of industry leaders, progressively taking action to adapt and thrive. Through partnering in this research project and through the Press Club initiative, they explored various potential revenue streams, including events, e-newsletters, and memberships.

"It's way easier to sell advertising, take legals," Joey said of the less-scrappy, more traditional approach.

> If that was still working, every publisher in the country would still live in the biggest house in town and have money to throw around. But that's not true anymore. … The days of supplementing the news primarily with advertising and legals is a dying business model. It just is, and it's not by choice. The choice is being made for us.

Joey, for one, firmly believes that reader-driven revenue is, at least, part of the solution to the new financial reality. "We believe that more and more revenues need to come from the reader for news in our community," he said. And higher subscription rates are one important aspect of the overall increase in reader revenue.

After the year of conversations with community residents, after the careful financial assessment, and after the porch summit at Adam's house, Joey was at ease with their business decisions (Figure 6.2). "At the end of the day, it's like any other business," he explained.

> You put it out into the public, your product, you charge what you think is fair, that you can make a living doing it. And the community decides whether they want to support your business. Not every restaurant makes it. Not every newspaper in this country's going to make it. That's the truth.

Figure 6.2 From left, Joey Young, Adam Strunk, Bruce Behymer, and Lindsey Young gather at the back of their office in June 2023 before attending a Press Club mingle one year after launching the membership model. Courtesy of Teri Finneman.

> You can either go out of business doing nothing, doing exactly what you're doing right now, or you can charge more, or come up with an event, or try something different. And you still might go out of business, that's the truth. But at least you tried something. Isn't that worth doing?

That said, Lindsey and Joey wholeheartedly understand the reservations their peers may have about taking such a leap. "A lot of this has just been a leap of faith, as far as, if you build it, will they come type thing," Lindsey said.

> It's just every time we have a mingle, I have that moment where I'm like, "Is anyone gonna show up, or am I gonna be eating all of these little cookies over the next week?" … And, so, I think some of the challenge is just, you know, taking that deep breath and being like, "It's cool. We're gonna try this, and we're gonna see what happens."

Joey, equally aware of the daunting nature of these bold steps, offered this advice to peers.

> I can totally see where a rural publisher who is, by the way, he is a working editor and publisher, he sells the ads and he might have just a little bit of help, would find this incredibly overwhelming. … And what I would say to them is pick one or two things. Don't do it all. Pick something that could help enhance the weekly paper.

His counsel is clear: Pick something, pick anything. "The longer we sit around and we rely on ROP print advertising and legals as our primary source of revenue, the longer we put off going out of business."

Not even 40 years old, Joey, already a seasoned veteran in the publishing business, adopts a broad perspective on his enterprise. "We have to have this paper sustain us for a long time," he said.

> We don't get to sell it in a year or two or just shut it down and retire. We don't get to do that. We have to have this thing sustain. So, investing a little bit of time, which I would say has been the case. We have not spent hours and hours and hours every day or every week working on all of this. We've fit it into stuff that we're already doing.

While revenue certainly stands as a primary reason to take bold action – altering organizational strategy, even overhauling the business model – it is not the sole reason. "The biggest reason to do it might be revenue," Joey said,

> but the secondary reason is that people love you for it. 'Oh, man. That was so much fun. … And, so, if they have fun at one of our events and they get to know everyone on staff, it's really beneficial from a readership standpoint.

The final piece of data collection for this book, the final oral history interview, was with Joey. Having journeyed through this research project, through a year of experimentation, and through ceaseless introspection on his business and the industry, Joey was asked for advice to other rural newspaper publishers. "Well, we made it the full year," our first author stated at the end of the final interview. "I will open the floor for any final reflections you have as we wrap this up." Presented here, in their entirety, are the final words from Joey for this project:

> The one thing I'm going to say is, is that this isn't a year-long experiment. Um, I'm overweight, I am. I'm a fat guy. I'm trying to lose weight. I've lost 50 pounds in the last year and a half. But what they say about losing weight is you can go on a fad diet, and you can lose a lot of weight all at once, but if you go off that fad diet, you gain it back. It's about lifestyle choices. You have to change how you live to lose weight. That's how this experiment works. We're changing how we live. We're changing how we operate. This is about sustainable paths forward. This isn't about a fad get rich quick scheme. This isn't about making a bunch of money this year. This is about changing how we focus the business and how we operate on a healthier basis. It works with weight loss; it'll work with your business. I'm not there yet from a weight loss standpoint or from a business standpoint, but this doesn't end in a year. This is something that you have to commit to. … I hope that I'll be able to check in in a year from now and say, "Hey, here's where we are after two years, here's what we're doing after three years, here's what we're doing after four years." This isn't like an experiment that ends after a year. This is a lifestyle choice for us in a lot of ways. After doing this for a year, we see the results, and we're going to continue forward. That's the big thing.

Reviving Rural News set out to provide a template for weekly newspapers around the world to help evolve their business model. Kansas Publishing Ventures essentially built the plane while flying it to learn lessons to make it easier for other publishers. To be sure, the experiment found that owners of multiple newspapers may want to focus on changes at one newspaper at a time. The same model that works in one community may not work in another, as evidenced by the slower progress in Hillsboro. The particulars of the Press Club model outlined in this book need to be taken into consideration with the needs and personality of individual communities. Those wanting to start small could still launch a membership program called Press Club but instead do something as simple as T-shirts, coffee mugs, or an annual luncheon in return for a membership fee.

Overall, the first year of *Harvey County Now* adopting new revenue streams was a modest success with $10,000 in additional profit. However, the groundwork of that first year that led the newsroom to feel comfortable expanding

Press Club to its entire subscription base has the potential for $230,000 in new revenue in Year 2. *Harvey County Now* continues to sell advertising and maintain its prior business model. Yet the enhancements that memberships, e-newsletters, and events have brought to not only its bottom line but also to its relationship with its community illustrate that innovation doesn't have to be difficult to be successful.

References

Abernathy, P. M. (2018). *The expanding news desert*. University of North Carolina. https://www.cislm.org/wp-content/uploads/2018/10/The-Expanding-News-Desert-10_14-Web.pdf

Barrett, M., Davidson, E., Prabhu, J., & Vargo, S. L. (2015). Service innovation in the digital age: Key contributions and future directions. *MIS Quarterly*, *39*(1), 135–154.

Christensen, C. M. (2013). *The innovator's dilemma: When new technologies cause great firms to fail*. Harvard Business Review Press.

Crocitto, M., & Youssef, M. (2003). The human side of organizational agility. *Industrial Management & Data Systems*, *103*(6), 388–397.

Deuze, M. (2008). The professional identity of journalists in the context of convergence culture. *Observatorio (Obs*)*, *2*(4), 103–117.

Ferrucci, P. (2018). "We've lost the basics": Perceptions of journalism education from veterans in the field. *Journalism & Mass Communication Educator*, *73*(4), 410–420.

Ferrucci, P., & Alaimo, K. I. (2020). Escaping the news desert: Nonprofit news and open-system journalism organizations. *Journalism*, *21*(4), 489–506.

Ferrucci, P., & Kuhn, T. (2022). Remodeling the hierarchy: An organization-centric model of influence for media sociology research. *Journalism Studies*, *23*(4), 525–543.

Ferrucci, P., & Perreault, G. (2022). Local is now national: *The Athletic* as a model for online local news. *New Media & Society*, 1–17. https://doi.org/10.1177/14614448221117748

Ganguly, A., Talukdar, A., & Kumar, C. (2022). Absorptive capacity and disruptive innovation: The mediating role of organizational agility. *IEEE Transactions on Engineering Management*, 1–12.

Griffin, R. (2018). Local news is dying, and it's taking small town America with it. *Bloomberg*. https://www.bloomberg.com/news/articles/2018-09-05/local-news-is-dying-and-it-s-taking-small-town-america-with-it

Gynnild, A. (2014). Journalism innovation leads to innovation journalism: The impact of computational exploration on changing mindsets. *Journalism*, *15*(6), 713–730.

Lewis, S. C., & Usher, N. (2013). Open source and journalism: Toward new frameworks for imagining news innovation. *Media, Culture & Society*, *35*(5), 602–619.

Matherly, T., & Greenwood, B. N. (2021). No news is bad news: Political corruption, news deserts, and the decline of the fourth estate. Academy of Management Proceedings. https://doi.org/10.5465/AMBPP.2021.10153abstract

Skocpol, T. (2003). *Diminished democracy: From membership to management in American civic life* (Vol. 8). University of Oklahoma Press.

Stinchcombe, A. L. (1965). Social structure and organizations. In J. March (Ed.), *Handbook of organizations* (pp. 153–193). Rand McNally.

Voakes, P. S. (1999). Civic duties: Newspaper journalists' views on public journalism. *Journalism & Mass Communication Quarterly*, *76*(4), 756–774.

Index

Note: Page references in *italics* denote figures and in **bold** tables.

For Product Safety Concerns and Information please contact our EU representative GPSR@taylorandfrancis.com
Taylor & Francis Verlag GmbH, Kaufingerstraße 24, 80331 München, Germany

www.ingramcontent.com/pod-product-compliance
Lightning Source LLC
LaVergne TN
LVHW010937110826
845149LV00013B/2645

* 9 7 8 1 0 3 2 5 3 9 7 7 5 *